TIMES
CHANGE:

A History of the Network of
Sacred Heart Schools

TIMES
CHANGE:

A History of the Network of
Sacred Heart Schools

Susan Putman Maxwell, RSCJ

TIMES CHANGE: A HISTORY OF THE NETWORK OF SACRED HEART SCHOOLS

iUniverse books may be ordered through booksellers or by contacting:

iUniverse
1663 Liberty Drive
Bloomington, IN 47403
www.iuniverse.com
1-800-Authors (1-800-288-4677)

ISBN: 978-1-5320-2872-4 (sc)
ISBN: 978-1-5320-2873-1 (e)

Print information available on the last page.

iUniverse rev. date: 08/03/2017

Times change, and we must change too.
~ Saint Madeleine Sophie Barat
To Saint Rose Philippine Duchesne
November 30, 1831 ~

TABLE OF CONTENTS

INTRODUCTION

After serving as Director of the Network of Sacred Heart Schools from 1984 to 1995, I was delighted to serve for twelve years as Director of Schools at Sacred Heart Schools in Chicago (Sheridan Road). Not only was I back in my hometown and close to family members, but I was gifted with the opportunity to lead in the spirit of the Goals and Criteria. After those wonderful years, I was called to serve on the Provincial Team and moved to St. Louis, where our Provincial offices are located. With some distance from the frenetic pace of our schools, I began to ponder a key reality: that by that time (2009) *thousands* of students had been educated according to the mission of the Society of the Sacred Heart as expressed in the Goals and Criteria. I came to realize that the story of the Network's evolution and early days was a unique one to tell. Therefore, when I completed my term on the Provincial Team, I stayed in St. Louis in order to be close to our archives so I could accurately document the story that I knew was important to be told.

Because of some medical challenges, this book has been slower in coming to completion than I would have liked; but every year has added new evidence that the decisions made over the years since Vatican II have proved both the strength of "the Church of the laity" and the depth of our mission statement, the Goals and Criteria. I write this mainly for all the lay colleagues who have joined us in Sacred Heart Schools as administrators, faculty and staff. So many are curious about our history, and what I present here may be of use to them in their work as educators of the Sacred Heart.

It is also important to me, very important, to express my gratitude here to Connie Solari, who has acted as my writing coach, cheerleader, critic and partner in this endeavor. I have known Connie for more than forty years. She began working at our Sacred Heart School in Atherton, California, in 1972, just as the Network was beginning to form; and I came to know her well when she served on the editorial board of *The Network Journal of Education* in the 1980s. While I was living in St. Louis, where I could access the provincial archives, we spoke weekly about the writing I had completed that week. It has been even more beneficial to meet with her weekly face to face ever since I arrived at our retirement facility on the property of our school in Atherton. I am also very grateful to the staff in our archives—Sisters Carolyn Osiek, Frances Gimber and Mary Louise Gavan, and Michael Pera. Each one provided me with invaluable resources. Finally, I want to thank the readers who provided insightful and encouraging feedback: Sisters Barbara Dawson, Mary Louise Gavan, Frances Gimber, Gail O'Donnell and Nance O'Neil.

As you will see, this book tells the story of the many, many people who brought this Network of Schools to its birth and strengthened it during its first twenty-five years. Having been a history major during my undergraduate years, I know that there is no such thing as unbiased history. And so this is *my* story of the birth of the Network of Sacred Heart Schools.

Susan Maxwell, RSCJ
Atherton, California

PART I

FROM VATICAN II TO THE GOALS AND CRITERIA

Chapter 1

Directives from the Church to the Society of the Sacred Heart

THE SOCIETY OF THE SACRED HEART

> *In her day as in ours there were more pressing needs: mouths to be fed, bodies to be clothed, sick to be nursed, prisoners to be visited. Heroic Christians in every age have risen up to minister to all of these. Her call was to open schools. She did not address herself in the first place to the radical restructuring of society that was going on around her. No more than Jesus was she a revolutionary in this sense. What directly concerned her was that inner revolution, which is the one sure foundation for an order of justice and peace; that revolution for lack of which revolutionaries become the new oppressors; the inner revolution of the heart, of the heart that has been opened by the Spirit to the unconditional love of God and neighbor, a revolution less violent than that going on in the streets of Paris, but not less radical.*[1]

Madeleine Sophie Barat founded the Society of the Sacred Heart in 1800 in Paris, France.[2] For our purposes it is important to know that the Society was born out of the violence and suffering of the French Revolution and its

[1] From a talk given by Cora Brady, RSCJ, Manhattanville College, 1980.

[2] There exist several biographies of her as well as a novel based on her life. Some of the more recent publications in English include *Saint Madeleine Sophie Barat*, C.E. Maguire, RSCJ, Sheed and Ward, New York, 1960; *Saint Madeleine Sophie, Her Life and Letters*, Margaret Williams, RSCJ, Herder and Herder, New York, 1965;

aftermath. As a young girl, Sophie received a rigorous, classical education under the tutelage of her older brother, Louis, who eventually became a Jesuit priest. She excelled in her studies and spoke and read several languages by the age of sixteen. Sophie initially felt called to be a Carmelite religious, but was drawn to a more active life, longing to give witness to her two abiding passions and convictions: the belief that God is a loving God, not the angry, judgmental God that was so often portrayed in her day; and the reality that girls could be educated in a challenging, intellectual way, not simply in the domestic arts.

The Society of the Sacred Heart was founded as a semi-cloistered religious congregation, meaning that the lives of the sisters were "wholly contemplative and wholly apostolic."[3] Silence and a strict order of day were followed, and the religious spoke only as part of their apostolic life. The mission of the Society was, and continues to be, to glorify the Sacred Heart of Jesus, to show forth the Love of God. The original Constitutions[4] assert the following:

> The means which the Society adopts for the purpose of glorifying the Sacred Heart of Jesus are chiefly the following four: the education of children as boarders; the free instruction of poor children as day pupils; retreats offered to persons living in the world; and such contacts with people living outside our communities as spring necessarily from its work.

The first Sacred Heart school opened in 1801 in Amiens, France; and by the time Sophie died in 1865, there were Sacred Heart schools

---

Madeleine Sophie Barat, a Life, Phil Kilroy, Paulist Press, New York/Mahwah, N.J., 2000; and *Sophie's Fire*, Constance Solari, 2012.

[3] These words, which fully express St. Madeleine Sophie's intent, were first used by Sister Jeanne de Charry.

[4] Like every religious order, RSCJ live their lives according to their "constitutions." The original Constitutions of the Society of the Sacred Heart (written in 1815 and formally approved by Pope Leo XII in 1826) clearly express the vision of St. Madeleine Sophie and her plan concerning the nature, end, spirit and character of the Society. In 1982, after prolonged study and reflection by that year's General Chapter, the Society published a volume entitled *Constitutions*, which included a second part, written in accordance with the spirit of the Second Vatican Council. This two-part document was given official approbation by the Church on January 1, 1987.

throughout France as well as in Italy, Switzerland, Belgium, Algiers, England, Ireland, Spain, Holland, Germany, Cuba, Austria, Poland, South America and North America. Philippine Duchesne and her companions opened the first Sacred Heart school beyond France in 1818 in St. Charles, Missouri. This was also the first free school west of the Mississippi River in the United States. As schools continued to open across the globe, the order of day and course of study were uniform. The studies were serious, cultivating the minds as well as nourishing the spirits of women who would be devoted to the Sacred Heart of Jesus, a loving God; the students were also expected to perform good deeds in God's name. As foundations continued to multiply, Sophie saw the need for a greater degree of unity; and for this, she sought the approval of the Vatican. By 1826, through the Pope's formal approbation of its Constitutions, the Society of the Sacred Heart had received Rome's seal of approval.

In 1840, Sophie averted a potential schism within the Society deriving from a power struggle between the Vatican and the archbishop of Paris. Among other things, the Pope wanted the headquarters of the Society to be in Rome while the archbishop and many of his French colleagues wanted Sophie to be centered in Paris.[5] The religious lined up on either side of the controversy. But while her sisters pressured her to choose sides, Sophie refused to do so and was able to heal the breach. Over the course of her sixty-five years as Superior General, Sophie and the Society survived the regime of Napoleon, saw France undergo two more revolutions, and witnessed first-hand Italy's struggle to become a full-fledged nation.

---

[5] The situation, which was enormously complex and had roots going back to the Middle Ages, is scrupulously documented in Kilroy's biography. All of Sophie's closest advisors and associates were drawn into the conflict, whose ultimate resolution required the collaboration of three French bishops, eight Cardinals, Pope Gregory XVI, and a Minister of France—in conjunction with Sophie's steadfast prayer and refusal to bring the situation to an irresolvable crisis.

Sister Nancy Ghio with Villa Duchesne students, 1953

The Sacred Heart schools quickly earned an excellent reputation. For a variety of complex reasons, they became known for educating the social elite, but this was not at all Sophie's original intent. Quite the contrary, she dreamed of educating *all* children, regardless of their parents' financial means. From the beginning, for almost every new boarding school established, a corresponding "free" school was opened to provide the poorer children of the area with high-quality education that they would not otherwise have received.[6] In her biography of St. Madeleine Sophie, C.E. Maguire, RSCJ, offers the following description of the first Sacred Heart free school in Amiens:

> At the beginning of 1802, a single-roomed separate building nearby was hired as a school for poor children, and soon housed one hundred and sixty of them. This increased work the little community took in their stride. A frequently cited quotation of Sophie's is: "The children in the boarding schools are not without resources; their wealth will allow them to have a good

---

[6] On occasion, such free schools were opened specifically for the developmentally disabled or orphans.

education. But for the orphans, it is a total loss. Truly, the poor do not touch our lives enough."

As we shall see, however, such free schools did not ultimately survive in the United States.

THE IMPACT OF THE SECOND VATICAN COUNCIL

I entered the Society of the Sacred Heart in 1964, two years after the start of Vatican II. The Second Vatican Council was unquestionably the most significant event for the Roman Catholic Church and Roman Catholic theology in the twentieth century. Called by Pope John XXIII amidst the social optimism of the 1960s, the Council met in four sessions from October 1962 to December 1965 and constituted a watershed event for Roman Catholic believers. John XXIII's desire to update (*aggiornamento* in Italian) the Church was carried on by his successor, Paul VI, who replaced him in 1963 for the Council's final sessions. The Council sought to engage the modern world in a new and more positive fashion, creating tremendous consequences for the life of the Church. In order to understand the scope and nature of the Council's influence, it is helpful to consider Vatican II under three aspects: the new direction for the Church taken by the Council; the crisis and turmoil that followed; and the lasting significance and questions regarding the place of Vatican II in the history of Catholic and Christian theology. These three aspects clearly played themselves out within the Society of the Sacred Heart over the subsequent decades.

For the purpose of considering the impact of Vatican II on the life of the Society, three works of the Council are of particular interest and bear further study by interested readers. *Perfectae Caritatis*[7] *(Decree on Renewal of Religious Life,* 1965) established general principles to guide the renewal

---

[7] This document, as well as *Apostolicam Actuositatem,* and *Gaudium et Spes,* mentioned later in this chapter can be found on the Vatican website:
http://www.vatican.va/archive/hist_councils/ii_vatican_council/documents/vat-ii_decree_19651028_perfectae-caritatis_en.html
http://www.vatican.va/archive/hist_councils/ii_vatican_council/documents/vat-ii_decree_19651118_apostolicam-actuositatem_en.html
http://www.vatican.va/archive/hist_councils/ii_vatican_council/documents/vat-ii_const_19651207_gaudium-et-spes_en.html

of the great variety of religious congregations. Because of this wide array of religious orders—each with its different history, characteristics, customs and mission—the Vatican Council did not give specific, broad-based instructions. Rather, it left to each individual community the authority to determine what needed to be changed in accordance with the spirit of its founder, the needs of modern life, and the situations wherein the members lived and worked.

The period that followed was marked by a huge amount of experimentation. Many institutes replaced their traditional habits with more modern attire, experimented with different forms of prayer and community life, and adapted the term "obedience to a superior" to mean a form of consultation and discussion. A great number of religious left religious life entirely, and in subsequent decades there was a significant drop in the number of religious vocations in the West. These changes certainly occurred in the Society of the Sacred Heart.

A second Vatican II publication, *Apostolicam Actuositatem (Decree on Apostolate of the Laity,* 1965), argued that the laity have a very real role to play in the Church and should be encouraged to undertake roles previously performed solely by clergy and religious. We shall see that this endorsement of the place of the laity in the Catholic Church had a major, and I believe very positive, effect on the schools of the Sacred Heart in the United States.

Finally, *Gaudium et Spes (Pastoral Constitution on the Church in the Modern World,* 1965) decrees that "the joys and hopes, the grief and anguish of the people of our time, especially of those who are poor or afflicted, are the joys and hopes, the grief and anguish of the followers of Christ as well." Those who interpret the purpose of the Second Vatican Council as one of embracing the secular world use *Gaudium et Spes* as their foundational document.

In addition to these three documents, two specific directives of Vatican II had a major impact on the Society of the Sacred Heart. The first of these was the directive given to all religious congregations to return to the Gospel according to the spirit of their Founder in order to respond to the needs of the world. As mentioned previously, by the mid-1960s Sacred Heart schools in the United States had become highly respected academies, usually educating girls but by then even some boys from increasingly wealthy families. Although such families had entered the top tiers economically, their Catholic children were not always accepted into the most prestigious prep schools, especially on the East Coast. Therefore, they often enrolled their girls in Sacred Heart schools.[8]

The free schools, however, did not always succeed in this country, although some lasted until the early 1960s.[9] Critics claimed that operating academies and free schools on the same campus created class divisiveness and ran contrary to the American spirit. Some argued further that the parochial school system served this purpose of less expensive Catholic education.[10] Whatever the case may have been, some Sacred Heart leaders in the United States, in light of the Vatican II directive, became concerned when reviewing the original spirit and charism of St. Madeleine Sophie and how it was currently being lived in this country.

It might be instructive here to give an example of how Sacred Heart education was lived in the early days in this country in contrast to the academies of the 1960s. Nikola Baumgarten, in her excellent article for *Journey of the Heart* (a compendium of articles assembled in 2000 for the Society's bicentennial) writes of those early days:

> The Sisters of the Sacred Heart thus made a major contribution to the Republican ideal of universal schooling in St. Louis. The work of the order spanned the complete range of the city's population: blacks and whites, Protestants and Catholics, English and French speakers, rich and poor. For nearly a decade the sisters offered the only educational opportunities for black, orphaned and poor girls. The numbers when added up were impressive as well. In the summer of 1828, the five

---

[8] In 1962, Robert Kennedy came to represent his family for the dedication of the Kennedy Building at Manhattanville College of the Sacred Heart, our college located in Purchase, New York. In conversation with me before the dedication, he alluded to this reality, adding with pride that many of his sisters had attended Sacred Heart schools, as had their mother.

[9] For example, Annunciation Parish School, New York City (1850-1952) and St. Katharine's Parish School, Philadelphia (1865-1961).

[10] Parochial schools are those supported and maintained by a religious body. The most numerous parochial schools in the United States are those operated under the auspices of the Roman Catholic Church.

schools of the Society in the city of St. Louis[11] included over one hundred girls and young women; in May 1832, attendance was close to 150 and by 1839, the combined enrollment of the Academy, day school, free school, Sunday school for blacks, and the orphanage well exceeded 200. This was a significant size, given that St. Louis' white student population only totaled about 1000 in that year.

Statistics such as these caused some Sacred Heart leaders in this country in the 1960s to reflect deeply on our mission and how it had evolved over time.

But I move forward too swiftly.

While discussion of the character of the U.S. schools was beginning to occur, life in the noviceship—where we received our initial formation as Religious of the Sacred Heart for two and one half years—was proceeding much as it had since the days of Sophie. We lived a structured day with specified times of prayer, including morning meditation, daily Mass, the chanting of the Office three times a day, the examen at noon, afternoon adoration in the chapel and night prayers. Our daily routine also included various household assignments and a rule of silence. The order of day was indeed silent, clear and consistent. Little did we know that a second directive from Vatican II would change that life profoundly. This directive offered a clear mandate that if we were to continue as educators, we had to live a fully apostolic life, not one that was semi-cloistered—not, in other words, the life we had learned so well in the noviceship.

At this same time, the international Society was playing a critical role in our lives. Since St. Madeleine Sophie's time, periodic "General Chapters" have been called in order to gather representatives from all parts of the world to set the course for the Society, in the light of the Constitutions, for the period of time before the next General Chapter (formerly six years). In attendance are the Superior General and her council, the Provincial of each geographic region or province, and, since 1967, elected delegates with the number determined by the number of sisters in each Province. To this day delegates to General Chapters consider both the challenges facing

---

[11] The reference here is to five distinct programs for different populations in one institution, the Convent of the Sacred Heart.

the Society and the opportunities present to give new life to its charism. In 1967, a Special Chapter was called only three years after the General Chapter of 1964. With hindsight, this unusual occurrence should be no surprise: the Vatican Council had directed the Society, in view of our work of education, to lift cloister and all that accompanied it. But at the time it was extraordinary.

These directives of Vatican II meant an end to cloister[12] and all that it meant in our daily lives. They also called for a profound examination of how authentically we were living our mission. These were indeed radical directives, calling for a summit of the Society's leaders from around the world.

At this time, I was a member of the New York Province, and our vicar[13] was Reverend Mother Helen Fitzgerald, a highly respected and insightful leader whose intuition helped us to make the necessary changes called for by the Church, difficult as those changes might have been for her. As is still the custom, she called for a Vicariate Chapter to prepare for the Special Chapter to be held in Rome. The radical nature of the impending changes is recorded in Ruth Cunningham's biography of Mother Fitzgerald, where she poignantly illustrates this most fundamental turning point in the life of the Society:

> When the Vicariate Assembly opened at Manhattanville on December 1, 1966, Mother Fitzgerald called for a very basic atmosphere of charity, of freedom, and more than anything else, of trust. . . . She listened to the views of others with great compassion, open, patient, strong. She spoke rarely during it, but at its close, her words were a premonition of what would be asked of the Society at the General Chapter, likening it to the piercing of the Heart of Christ:

---

[12] This occurred in 1964, although we did not hear of it until later.

[13] Prior to Vatican II and the Constitutions of 1982, the leader of each geographic area of the Society of the Sacred Heart was called a Vicar. In that role the Vicar needed to refer to the Superior General for any serious decision in her Vicariate. After the Vatican Council, the title Vicar shifted to Provincial, and her responsibilities became greater: Provincials can make many decisions for their Provinces without obtaining the permission of the Superior General.

Many of us have felt that a sword was being put into the heart of the Society by all the new demands being put on religious life, because those of us who have lived it for years, and loved it and its structure, felt that it was almost sacrilegious to touch it. However, the Church has asked us to open up and go out more and give the Heart of Christ more to others.

As a woman who was as inserted in the wider world as was possible in her cloistered lifestyle, Mother Fitzgerald saw that religious life had to change if it was to survive. At the same time she knew her sisters in the Society of the Sacred Heart very well and understood that the next few years were bound to be difficult in one way or another for all of them. At the age of seventy-one, she put aside her own love of silence and cloister and the beautiful order of a structured religious house, and worked for the changes that the present required. Sister Ann Conroy commented eloquently on Mother Fitzgerald's love of the past Society and the profound difficulty these changes must have presented to her: She was happy with the Society as it was. There was a dignity about it that matched her dignity; there was an order to it; there was a clarity—and she felt that it was a very effective group. She knew it would not be able to live if it continued in the old ways, and the life of the Society was more important to her than the things she held dear.[14]

The calling of this special Chapter in 1967 is the most powerful indication of the upheaval in the Society after the changes called for by Vatican II. A further indicator is the fact that at this Chapter, the Superior General of the Society resigned, a heretofore unheard of event. From the founding of the Society, superiors general were elected for life, so her action was a significant break with tradition. Out of respect, those of us who were not in attendance at the Chapter were given very little information or details of this resignation other than the fact that it took place. Thus, I was touched and taken aback when in 1973, during the preparation for my final commitment to the Society in Joigny,[15] Sister Rebecca Ogilvie Forbes

---

[14] *Helen Fitzgerald, RSCJ, 1895-1982*, by Ruth Cunningham, RSCJ.
[15] The birthplace of St. Madeleine Sophie in Burgundy, France.

asked to see me. She had been the Vicar of the Vicariate of England/Wales during the Chapter of 1967. She wanted me to know that the night before this historic resignation and in the midst of confusion and controversy, she and Sister Fitzgerald had pledged their commitment to accept the resignation of the Superior General by exchanging their profession rings. She also told me that Sister Fitzgerald had played an important leadership role at that General Chapter.

I knew Sister Fitzgerald well. It was she who had accepted me into the Society; and during my final year at Manhattanville College, she was living on campus and we had enjoyed many conversations together. I knew what this exchange of rings must have represented for a woman who was watching an entire way of life begin to slip away. What this sense of loss and chaos would evolve into was a mystery to us all. But a suggestion of it was present in a statement she had made at the New York Province Chapter of 1966:

> It is hard for some of us, and less hard for others, but with the Society we should give what we have. . . . We have been given the love of His Heart, and we have been so happy with it. Our Lord seems to be saying: "Go out now, and give it; make my Heart known, forgetting about yourselves."[16]

---

[16] Cunningham, *op. cit.*

CHAPTER 2

Mission Considerations
and School Closings

THE CHAPTER OF 1967

Sister Fitzgerald predicted accurately that the Special Chapter of 1967 would mark a major turning point in the life of the Society of the Sacred Heart. The long and densely written Chapter document, *Orientations* ad experimentum, bears witness to this fact.[17]

Following the directives of Vatican II, the Society of the Sacred Heart, as did other religious orders, entered into a period of experimentation. It is difficult to choose significant quotations from the documents of the 1967 Chapter for our purposes here because there are so many. But the following paragraphs, from the rather rambling opening section of the document, which deals explicitly with the internal life of the religious, provide good examples of the spirit and content of this Special Chapter:

> One of the duties of the Chapter is to remove anything that prevents our responding effectively to the call of the Church: identification with particular social classes, triumphalism, an

---

[17] Chapter documents represent the concluding statements after the Chapter delegates have met for anywhere from six weeks to two months. They are sent to each member of the Society of the Sacred Heart around the world, and the insights and conclusions in these documents indicate the direction the members are to take in the coming years. They vary in length, strength and clarity from Chapter to Chapter. All Chapter documents are available in the Provincial Archives in St. Louis.

---

air of self-satisfaction, the tendency to stress structures rather than persons, and a certain lack of charity among ourselves. Charity must be the centre of our renewal, since the witness we are called upon to give beyond every other is the WITNESS TO LOVE. . . . To regroup our forces and go to those less favoured with this world's goods, we will have to suppress some works that are no longer fruitful and even sometimes those in full activity but less necessary, in order to develop centres of education in the 'slums' or in small villages where the need for a Christian education is more gravely felt.

Thus, the Chapter was calling us to examine our own lives before reviewing and clarifying how we were living the mission through the ministries that St. Madeleine Sophie had outlined so clearly for us. We were called to renew our mission of "showing forth the love of God" and to embrace that love as the core of our lives with one another and with those we were serving of all classes and races.

In calling the leaders of the Society to examine the work of our schools in the light of our original charism, many of the statements from the Special Chapter of 1967 had major effects on some of the leaders of the Society in the United States. I knew several RSCJ in leadership positions who felt called to live the commitment to the poor that St. Madeleine Sophie experienced so deeply. In her day, the means to do this was to found free schools. The leaders I knew were trying to find an appropriate way to live this part of our charism in twentieth-century America. At the same time, of course, there were other insightful leaders who believed that what we were doing in our schools with middle-class and upper-middle-class students could ultimately do more than anything else to empower the poor.

The following quotation from the section of the Chapter of 1967 documents entitled *Apostolic Life* provides a strong introduction to this lengthy section. Rather than looking back to the time of St. Madeleine Sophie, as we were prone to do, it speaks to the need for constant movement forward, a need to renew our approach to educating students:

Education helps man[18] to know himself and makes it possible for him to forge his own destiny. The human race is confronted today with the immense problem of development in all its forms. God's plan in salvation history is written in the heart of the continuous movement of evolution. It is our responsibility to understand the meaning of our mission in a pluralist and secularist world, which is moving towards Christ and where, more and more, we realize the worth of the human person. In this light, we should undertake the renewal and adaptation of our work of education.

By this time the insights and writings of Teilhard de Chardin, S.J. were having an impact on well-educated Catholics, and this quotation clearly echoes his belief that the world is moving towards Christ rather than resting in a place of immovable beliefs, traditions and customs. It is noteworthy that this document, written in 1967, speaks of evolution in such a positive light.

The Chapter document also spoke of the humanizing mission of education—the fact that the contemporary world features a population that is becoming increasingly aware of its potential. In this same vein, it spoke to the need for a relational, student-centered approach to education.

In a world where man is becoming more and more conscious of his own worth, *education* acquires a fundamental importance since by it man becomes man.

In a world where interpersonal relations are becoming increasingly important, one of the first roles of education is to enable man to *dialogue*.

Class discussions thus became an increasingly important part of the curriculum and methodology as I entered my first classrooms in Bloomfield Hills, Michigan. Education in general was continuing to shift from an emphasis on learning facts and figures in an often rote manner to an emphasis on teaching students to think for themselves—a quality that had long been a hallmark of Sacred Heart education. True to the spirit of St.

---

[18] One must allow here and elsewhere in the document for the androcentric language of the time.

Madeleine Sophie, we were teaching students to express themselves clearly and well and with self-confidence.

Historically Sacred Heart education was known for the strength of its humanities programs. This centerpiece of the high school curriculum had included grammar, social studies, rhetoric, religious education, logic, literature, Latin and French. During the late 1960s and 1970s, math and science became stronger components of the curriculum, and the interdisciplinary thrust that had always characterized a Sacred Heart education now folded in these strengthened elements as well. In the words of the Chapter document:

> In a world of *scientific and technical progress,* it is more and more necessary that Christian educators do not create a parallel world, but, by taking part in progress, contribute to the building of the body of Christ.

In effect, the "world of scientific and technical progress" was now seen to be a key part of our curriculum and would henceforth be in dialogue with all other subjects.

The Chapter documents brought about other key changes in our schools in the United States, notably attempts to offer Sacred Heart education to students who would not otherwise have had access to it. In Bloomfield Hills, we had the great advantage of enrolling students from a summer program, the Sacred Heart Enrichment Program (SHEP) begun by Sister Annette Zipple, which took place for several years at our school across town in Grosse Pointe, Michigan. This program prepared capable middle-school students from inner city Detroit to enroll in our high school in Grosse Pointe as well as our school in Bloomfield Hills and other excellent high schools. Our suburban students welcomed those from the city, and there is no question that they added a great deal to the school community. Similar programs were initiated in other U.S. Sacred Heart schools after Vatican II. It is clear that many statements from the Chapter of 1967, such as the one that follows here, proved to be powerful catalysts for change in our schools and connected us with major cultural shifts taking place in this country in the 1960s.

> In a world which longs for the universal brotherhood of man, the Society, faithful to the words of Christ "You are all brothers" (Mt. 23:8), convinced that this union among men is accomplished above all by education, should do everything in its power to bring about the *fusion of classes* and the *equality of races*.

Another catalyzing quote focused on the role of the laity within our schools and the participation of our teachers in outside educational organizations:

> The Society will collaborate with other educational organizations. It will integrate lay people into its apostolic work, recognizing that this means that we must admit them to the same level as religious in administrative functions, listen to them, recognize their right to vote and use their initiative.

From the vantage point of 2016 and the leadership of Pope Francis in the Catholic Church, it is abundantly clear that the previously mentioned Vatican II document on the laity was prophetic. Certainly, there had been some lay teachers in each of our schools before Vatican II, but the past forty years have witnessed the inspiring and truly life-giving role of the laity within our Network of Sacred Heart Schools. Their place on faculties and staffs, as well as boards of trustees, has enabled this education to flourish into the twenty-first century. The integration of the laity into key roles within Sacred Heart education has been organic and deeply influential.

In an article he wrote for a 1988 RSCJ Newsletter, one of our original lay trustees, Donat Marchand from the Convent of the Sacred Heart in Greenwich, Connecticut, made this very point:

> Given our responsibility as Christians, is there a way other than as guardians of the Sacred Heart tradition in education by which so few of us can have so much influence on so many? The tradition of Sacred Heart education was preserved through the 19th century and most of the 20th century almost exclusively through the efforts of the members of the Society of the Sacred Heart. The challenge before us, lay and religious, is to preserve the tradition beyond the boundaries of the 20th century, and

even the 21st. If we are to live up to the challenge, it will depend
upon a true partnership of lay and religious men and women. I
trust that each of us, lay and religious, will rise to the challenge.

The profound and eloquent truth within his words is apparent almost
thirty years later as lay and religious continue to build the legacy of Sacred
Heart education.

The lifting of cloister and the partnership with the laity also led Sacred
Heart educators in the United States to involve themselves in national and
regional organizations such as the National Association of Independent
Schools and the Association for Supervision and Curriculum Development.
Up until the 1960s, RSCJ participation in such organizations had been
the purview of those of us who were working in one of our colleges. Now,
because of the impact of Vatican II, Religious of the Sacred Heart from our
academies began to play key roles in national educational organizations.
Some of us served on the boards of both regional organizations of
independent schools, e.g., ISACS (Independent Schools Association of the
Central States), as well as national ones, e.g., NAIS (National Association
of Independent Schools).

Some people maintain that the Chapter statement cited above, as well
as the Vatican II document on the laity, was necessary because there were
fewer and fewer men and women entering religious life. But for those of us
living through the past forty or more years in Catholic schools, it is obvious
that our lay colleagues have brought gifts from the worlds of education,
finance, law, construction and the like, as well as a serious commitment
to Sacred Heart education.

Just as the document that emerged from the Special Chapter of 1967
called for greater inclusion of lay people, so did it call for educators to
educate students to a sense of their place within a world community:

> In a world which is working towards the unity of the human
> family, we must *go beyond local and national spirit* to help one
> another and understand the needs of different countries.
> In a world where hunger and ignorance can be overcome only
> by education, we should ask ourselves: if our pupils leave us
> with a real sense of social justice and the determination to work

to change the world; and if we ourselves educate the children who have the greatest need of us.

As we shall see, one of the first programs initiated by our Network of schools was an active student exchange program among our Sacred Heart schools worldwide. Such connections have flourished since then in many different and creative ways. Ideally such exchange experiences lead our students to a greater first-hand awareness of the needs of the larger world—and to a habit of asking themselves the same questions as those addressed by the 1967 Chapter documents. As was true for St. Madeleine Sophie, such crucial questions are foremost in the minds and hearts of Sacred Heart educators. We are always striving to achieve more with our students in this important area, and we can point with pride to our graduates: So many of their lives are filled with a commitment to social justice.

Finally, the Chapter documents of 1967 posed crucial questions regarding the very nature of our apostolic work and the way in which we had accomplished it for over 150 years:

> In a world where the Church calls us to new tasks, we must give to education its full present-day dimension. Without prejudice to existing work, the criteria for our choice among all these forms of apostolate should be: better service; more pressing need; universal good; and wider vision.
> In a world which is moving towards socialization of education, the Society ought constantly to re-evaluate its raison d'être in the light of its mission.

THE CHAPTER OF 1970 AND SCHOOL CLOSINGS

It is important to repeat here that the Special Chapter of 1967 was a time of emotion and turmoil for all in attendance. After the historic resignation of the Superior General, the delegates elected a new Superior General who was to serve for the three years before the upcoming General Chapter of 1970. There is no question that the Chapter of 1967 planted seeds for other profound changes in the Society. We in the United States began to move towards painful decisions to close some of our schools. But at the same time, life-giving seeds were also planted for the creation of our Network of Sacred Heart Schools.

But again, I jump ahead.

Suddenly, as we moved into the period of experimentation mandated by the directives of Vatican II and made specific by our Special Chapter of 1967, everything began to change. Gone was the uniform order of day for every Religious of the Sacred Heart in any part of the world. Gone was the uniform curriculum in every Sacred Heart school. No longer could a diplomat who was transferred from France to Ireland enroll his daughter in a Sacred Heart school and know that she would find herself in a familiar environment.

It must be admitted that experimentation and creativity were flourishing in some schools, while others tried to continue under the familiar regularity of the days before Vatican II. But in the midst of such historic and frequently difficult decisions, there was an experience of new life, energy, hope, and expectation, particularly among those of us who were newer to the Society. I was happily teaching, serving as Dean of Students and then Head of the High School in Bloomfield Hills, Michigan—and energized by our many commitments in the Society to change the world. I remember vividly an assembly of the former New York Province when a proposal was brought forward that we should take it upon ourselves "to end poverty, racism and violence." We all voted enthusiastically to do so, and I think we truly believed this would happen. In this atmosphere of energetic confidence—and as we shall see as well, out of the pain of some school closings—the Network of Sacred Heart Schools was born.

At this time, there were five Provinces in the United States, each with its own Provincial who served as leader for the sisters in her geographic area. With so much change—some might argue chaos!—in the Catholic Church after the Vatican Council, the Provincials in 1969 formed a group called the Interprovincial Board, or the IPB. Designed to further unity (one could even say union) among the national schools and other Society services, the IPB consisted of the five Provincials, one additional representative from each Province, and administrative staff with expertise in various areas of governance. Thus began the national conversations among the Sacred Heart Provincials that were to culminate in the creation of one United States Province in 1982. Together they discussed national topics such as the appointment of the Mistress of Novices and the possibility of national financial planning, as well as the future of Sacred Heart schools in the United States. In fact, the Southern Province had already closed its City House in St. Louis in 1968. In 1969, the Society withdrew from our school in Grosse Pointe, Michigan, and the local Board of Trustees took over the school. For a variety of complex reasons, some other institutions were selected for closing.

Just as the IPB members were settling into this new mode of joint planning and decision-making, the international Society once again came to the forefront, calling us all to new understandings of religious life and our chosen ministries. These new understandings were to become clear at the General Chapter of 1970, a chapter that played a very significant role in the worldwide Society of the Sacred Heart. Indeed, with hindsight, a critical role.

More succinct and focused than the *Orientations* ad Experimentum of the Chapter of 1967, the documents of the 1970 Chapter would undoubtedly be of interest to many readers. Of particular interest here, as the Network of Sacred Heart Schools neared its birth, are the five "options"[19] adopted at this Chapter. These options outlined the "next steps" for all Religious of the Sacred Heart and acted as mandates for their leaders:

> 1) An international community, one and necessarily pluriform, we want to live our new awareness of this communion, and to accept the practical consequences of co-responsibility and sharing at the international level.
>
> 2) At a time when the integral development of man is a task of special urgency, we reaffirm our educational mission as our service in the Church. Turned towards the future, we must bring all our creativity to bear on this Mission. It is the love of Christ which urges us to meet the needs of those weighed down by ignorance or servitude, and above all, the needs of the young who search for meaning in their life. *Let us educate to a faith which will be relevant in a secularized world, to a deep respect for intellectual values, and to a social awareness which will impel to action.* In this perspective, we wish to examine seriously

---

[19] The word "option" in this context best translates as a "direction" or "call."

the apostolic value of our institutions and to take appropriate action.[20] [my italics]

3) In the light of the Gospel and of our social context, we wish to stand in solidarity with the poor.

4) At a time when mankind hungers and thirsts for justice, our attitude must be one of solidarity with the Third World, which suffers poverty and oppression.

5) We therefore commit ourselves to the renewal, at depth, of our life as a community, convinced that this is the one condition essential to the future of our religious life and to a genuine response to the summons of the Church and the world.

At this point, the general consensus was that with diminishing resources of both sisters and finances, some of our schools would have to be closed. Many who were aware of what was being discussed by our leaders felt that this was the only way in which we might provide the very best in Sacred Heart education within the remaining schools. We also felt called to extend our ministries *beyond* our schools in order to fulfill our mission more authentically, as determined by St. Madeleine Sophie and the Chapters of 1967 and 1970. During this time, each Province in the United States hired a management consulting firm to help with its decision-making. Thus continued the agonizing process of determining which other schools in the United States would have to close. From the vantage point of 2015, it seems fair to say that the documents of the Chapters of 1967 and 1970, as well as the prevailing energy of those who had attended those chapters, drove the life of the Society in the ensuing years.

In the end, between 1968 and 1972, almost a third of our Sacred Heart schools in the United States[21] were closed, with the deep pain of

---

[20] I include more detail concerning the second option, which deals with mission, because these words will be so familiar to those who have lived with the Goals and Criteria for all the years since 1975.

[21] Between 1968 and 1975, we closed ten academies: City House and Barat Hall for Boys, St. Louis (1893-1968); Eden Hall, Torresdale, Pennsylvania (1847-1968); Overbrook, Philadelphia, Pennsylvania (1924-1969); Grosse Pointe Academy, Grosse Pointe, Michigan (1885-1969); Prince Street, Rochester, New York (1863-1969); Clifton Academy, Cincinnati, Ohio (1876-1970); Nottingham Academy, Buffalo, New York (1961-1972); Noroton Academy, Noroton, Connecticut (1924-1972); El Cajon Academy, El Cajon, California (1956-1972); Elmhurst Academy, Providence/

each situation experienced profoundly by religious, students and their families, alumnae/i, faculty, staff and friends. As previously noted, one of these schools was located in Grosse Pointe, Michigan, across town from those of us in Bloomfield Hills. We were required to attend the evening gathering at the War Memorial in Grosse Pointe when parents, faculty and staff were told that their school would close at the end of that academic year. The representative from the management consulting firm made the announcement, and the emotional outburst in that room stays with me to this day.

Portsmouth, Rhode Island (1872-1972); and Glen Oak Academy, Cleveland, Ohio (1964-1975).

CHAPTER 3

The Stuart Conferences and Move toward a Network

THE FIRST STUART CONFERENCES

There is considerable confusion about exactly when the Network of Sacred Heart Schools was born. Was it in 1972 when Sister Catherine (Kit) Collins was named the National Coordinator of Sacred Heart education? Or was it in the summer of 1969, when the first Stuart Conference took place at Barat College of the Sacred Heart in Lake Forest, Illinois?

In fact, there was confusion in so very many areas of our lives at this time. As cloister was lifted and we entered the post-Vatican II world, we also entered all the upheaval of the 1960s, from the assassinations of the Kennedys and Martin Luther King to the Vietnam War, to Johnson's War on Poverty, and to so many other key historic events of that era. Similarly, for a variety of reasons that can never be precisely formulated, sisters began to leave religious life, and far fewer women were entering the convent. When I arrived at the noviceship in Albany, New York, in 1964, there were seventy-seven novices where there had recently been more than one hundred. When I left Albany for Bloomfield Hills, Michigan, in 1967, there were only forty-three.

So, as we continue with this account of the development of the Network of Sacred Heart Schools and their Goals and Criteria, what might sound like continual, systematic listings of insights was anything but. Each of the gatherings that developed the eventual articulation of our convictions about education came with lively debate, differences of opinion, new insights, and finally some agreement.

A key series of such gatherings were the Stuart Conferences of 1969, 1971 and 1974. Initiated under the auspices of the IPB, these conferences were planned and executed by Sister Kit Collins working with a group of creative Sacred Heart educators called the Stuart Committee. Both the committee and the conferences were named after a famous English Sacred Heart educator of the late nineteenth and early twentieth century, Janet Erskine Stuart, RSCJ. It was, in short, exciting to experience educational gatherings, not just for those in the highest positions of authority, but for all of us.

Sister Collins had entered the Society of the Sacred Heart after graduating from Manhattanville College of the Sacred Heart. Her first ministry was teaching at Eden Hall, one of our schools in Philadelphia; she next served there as curriculum director. From 1968 to 1971, she was the Headmistress of Stone Ridge Country Day School of the Sacred Heart in Bethesda, Maryland. From 1971 to 1972, she served as Director of Education for the Washington Province. Thus, she was very well known to educators in our schools on the East Coast. She was not, however, particularly well known in the schools of the South, the Midwest or the West Coast. The Stuart conferences served to introduce her as a national educational leader.

At this first Stuart Conference in the summer of 1969, hundreds of educators, including faculty, staff and administrators, gathered to discuss the future of Sacred Heart education in the United States. Topics revolved around curriculum development for secondary-school educators and continuous progress education for those teaching in our elementary schools. Workshop leaders were drawn from Sacred Heart schools as well as other independent schools, colleges and public school districts. A sampling of leaders and their topics included the following: Dr. Allan A. Glatthorn, Principal of the Abington School in Pennsylvania, "A New Curriculum for a New Age"; Sister Athalie Joy, RSCJ, "The Buffalo Social Studies Curriculum and Project"; Sister Catherine Wulftange, SND, Xavier University, Cincinnati, Ohio, "Developing an Environment for Learning"; and Dr. Abraham S. Fischler, Dean of Graduate Studies, Nova University, Fort Lauderdale, Florida, "The Need for Individualization in Order to

Achieve Our Goals."[22] Thus, the planning committee offered workshops, innovative educational sessions and—perhaps above all—a sense of the unifying spirit of being part of a group that extended far beyond one's individual school. These were creative days characterized by lots of energy, while the leadership in the five Provinces was, of course, simultaneously adjusting to life after cloister.

In fact, the planning committee for the 1969 Stuart Conference received an extremely positive response from the six Provincials of the United States and Canada.[23] In a letter to the Stuart Committee, they stated with enthusiasm their appreciation for the "excellent and stimulating conference at Barat, which generated a true upsurge of thinking nationally and internationally in planning for the future."

Coming soon after the Stuart Conference of 1969, the 1970 General Chapter of the Society of the Sacred Heart proved to be a watershed event for the worldwide Society. The documents of this 1970 General Chapter complemented the discussions of the 1969 Stuart Conference and are quoted to this day in Sacred Heart schools around the world as part of the original articulation of the Goals and Criteria.[24]

One key statement reaffirmed the Society's educational mission within the historical context of the 1970s: "At a time when the integral development of man is a task of special urgency, we reaffirm our educational mission as our service in the Church."[25] Another statement explicitly articulated this mission's connectedness to the poor and marginalized: "In the light of the Gospel and of our social context, we wish to stand in solidarity with the poor."[26] There is no doubt that documents emerging from the 1970 Chapter encouraged the work begun at the first Stuart Conference of 1969 to move forward.

A second Stuart Conference was held in 1971 at another Sacred Heart College, Maryville in St. Louis, Missouri. Heads of School from both

---

[22] An interesting economic side note: the cost of room and board for participants was $3.00 per night!

[23] Sisters Mavie Coakley, Alice Amyot, Beth Nothomb, Elizabeth Cavanagh, Helen Sheahan and Elizabeth Sweeney.

[24] The 1975, 1990 and 2005 Goals and Criteria are included in their entirety in the Appendix to this work.

[25] 1970 Chapter document.

[26] Ibid.

Canada and the United States, together with many other Sacred Heart educators and the leadership of the six Provinces, attended this conference. At their next meeting, building on the General Chapter documents of 1970, the Heads of School, under the leadership of Sister Collins, began the slow process of articulating what they called *Objectives and Criteria for Sacred Heart Schools in North America*.[27] In this document, we can see early signs of what was to come in the Goals and Criteria of 1975. The perceptive reader will note that in all these discussions the participants seemed to use the words *goals*, *objectives*, and even *criteria* somewhat interchangeably.

Some of the key insights in 1971 called the schools to educate students to a sense of their own worth, and to do so with a diverse student body that would reflect the world in which these students were to live in the future. Being true to the insights and vision of St. Madeleine Sophie Barat, the schools were called to encourage a love of learning as well as an active concern for the poor, an awareness of the problems of the Third World, and a knowledge of international issues. The document goes on to say that it would be important for the wider community to perceive Sacred Heart schools as both God-centered and welcoming of students of all denominations and faiths. Balancing these values within the culture of the school would require an atmosphere of very real trust and respect for one another. As one of our schools stated many years later at the end of its strategic plan, a fundamental hope would be that those who got to know this particular Sacred Heart school would exclaim, "See how they love one another!"

It was clear that in order to achieve these goals or objectives, some specific criteria would have to be in place. These would include, but not be limited to, an admissions process enabling families to understand the goals of the school; a strong financial aid program; a clear introduction and ongoing education of faculty and staff to the values of the school; staff-student and student-student relationships that evidence openness, mutual respect, and concern for one another; and evidence from the alumnae/i that the school's objectives had influenced their lives.

Certainly all of these discussions, conferences and national gatherings pointed the way towards the importance of national leadership. Thus, after the 1971 Stuart Conference, and after having seen her strong leadership

---

[27] Available in the provincial archives in St. Louis.

skills and educational vision in so many ways, the IPB named Sister Collins the National Coordinator for Sacred Heart Schools in 1972.

Years later, in 1990, Marina Chukayeff McCarthy, a graduate of Stone Ridge in Bethesda, Maryland, wrote her thesis for Harvard's Graduate School of Education on Sacred Heart education. She entitled it *The Anchor and the Wind: a Profile of Sacred Heart Schools in the U.S.* In it, she makes a very important point: "In a climate of much suspicion and distrust," she says of the late 1960s, "there emerged a person—an honest broker, if you will—who began to help the Order move itself forward: Catherine (Kit) Collins, RSCJ." She goes on to write, "Collins had credibility. This enabled her to serve as a negotiator—particularly between younger nuns who were suspicious of older ones and vice versa."

At the same time, we held very real affection and respect for one another and shared a conviction that the world, perhaps now more than ever, needed education that communicated clear values as well as rigorous academic content. The appointment of Sister Collins was our first experience of national leadership, cohesion and collaboration and certainly pointed the way towards unifying the five Provinces into one—a significant change that did not take place for another ten years.

The IPB, however, did recognize the importance of involving *all* RSCJ in this country in the articulation of our mission, not only those who were working in Sacred Heart schools. Thus, during the fall following the Stuart Conference of 1971, the five Provincials asked the communities to look ahead and formulate educational goals that would enable the Religious of the Sacred Heart in the United States to make known the love of God revealed in Christ. The priorities that had emerged from the General Chapter of 1970 provided the common base for the Society; the concrete means by which to implement the conclusions of the Chapter delegates, however, had been left to the Provinces. In inviting our contributions, the Provincials reminded us of the significant remarks made by Mother Bultó, Superior General, at the opening session of the 1970 General Chapter.[28] "Everyone in the Society is watching us—some with anxiety, others with great hope—looking to us for clear, calm, bold direction to draw us together and to give us courage to go forward." She then raised the key

---

[28] Mother Bultó had been elected by the Chapter delegates in 1967 after the resignation of Reverend Mother Sabine de Valon.

question: "As Religious of the Sacred Heart, how can we, both by our life and by our work, convey to the world the message of the freely given love of God, which is revealed in His Son?"[29]

RATIONALE FOR A NETWORK

In the paper entitled *Compilation of Communities' Thinking on The Goals and Objectives, February 1972,*[30] we see two things: the responses to Mother Bultó's question from every RSCJ in the United States; and the results of the invitation from the IPB to every RSCJ to participate in the process of beginning to articulate what was to become the Goals and Criteria. The paper is long and rambling, but it is important to emphasize that *all* RSCJ participated, not just those in the schools. Every word of input from the religious is included.

I find it striking that the Provincials highlight in their introduction that while all "goals" (again this word was used in a variety of ways in the period leading up to the final approval of the Goals and Criteria in 1975) are not of equal weight, all stem from our commitment to bring Christ's message to the world, and all hold in common that we can believe in the future. Of particular interest, I think, is their felt need to articulate that we *had* a future—because this was a real question at the time. Similarly, it is of great interest that the first "goal" they articulate is the following: "As a Society, to anticipate and adapt to change." Change had certainly not been a hallmark of the lives of the Religious of the Sacred Heart before Vatican II. It was, however, a keynote of the closing paragraph of the documents from the General Chapter of 1970:

> Thus, to remain faithful today is, in a sense, to change. It is to go beyond precise laws to rediscover their spirit and life. "The times change," wrote Saint Madeleine Sophie to Mother Duchesne in America in 1831, "and we must change too." For her the only thing necessary was to make known the love of God revealed in Christ. For us, too, this is the sole criterion of our renewal.

---

[29] 1970 Chapter document.

[30] Available in the provincial archives in St. Louis.

It is important also to remember that the five U.S. Provincials had all been at the General Chapter of 1970, a fact that resulted in the strong, clear language that formed the first Goals of the Goals and Criteria. At that Chapter in her opening remarks, Reverend Mother Bultó had also stated the following:

> Does the Gospel not always, does it not ever remain, the great innovation which upsets our routine, shows up our laziness, jolts our apathy? Unless we honestly meet this challenge of the Gospel, any action that we take will be superficial. We must have enough balance, courage and love to make the Society respond at a very deep level, with sincerity, and with one mind.

And further, consider this statement from the five Provincials in their introductory comments to the paper of February 1972 summarizing the input of all RSCJ in the United States:

> In this context, the goals and objectives can be read as expressing the thoughts of various religious as to what should be considered if we are serious about seeking not what confirms us in our present position, but rather something that looks beyond it. Although areas do overlap, the material has been divided into the following categories: apostolic community, education, internationality, the poor, the third world, government, communication.

There is no question that this paper was foundational when we began to articulate the Goals and Criteria in 1973.

In March of 1973, another very significant meeting of the Heads of School and other administrators took place in Washington, D.C. This gathering was entitled *One Step Forward Toward Justice*. From this meeting came the commitment that within the year every Sacred Heart School in the United States, including associated schools[31] where Religious of the Sacred Heart often worked in less advantaged neighborhoods, would

---

[31] The designation of an associate school depended on the inclusion of an RSCJ on a given school's faculty or staff. Thus, this designation varied from year to year. The listings in the RSCJ Directory of 1983-84 include the following associate schools: St. Madeleine Sophie School in El Cajon, California; Holy Redeemer School in

move "one step forward towards justice." They cited that each school would report progress at the end of the next academic year in at least one of the following five specific objectives:

1. Examine curriculum (understood as the way learning takes place) for possible traces of oppression and violence. Substitute a "redemptive system."
2. Administrative teams take one step forward toward the process of institutional self-renewal . . . for greater openness to the wider world.
3. Commit ourselves to continuing education of the multi-generational community.
4. Foster values by implementing specific *programs* in the schools.
5. Focus on bigger issues through study, experience, reflection. Education for a "thinking heart" that impels to action.[32]

In the midst of the contradictory realities of the pain of school closings and the sense of new life emerging in the Society in the United States, off I went in the summer of 1973 to prepare for and make my final profession in the Society of the Sacred Heart. Joining a group of RSCJ from many parts of the globe, I was part of a French-speaking program in Joigny, France, the birthplace of St. Madeleine Sophie Barat. Here I was to come face to face with the reality that RSCJ around the world had indeed emerged from cloister. I was also to meet with very strong anti-American thoughts and feelings. Vivid in my memory is the day I stood and announced to the group of more than forty sisters gathered there that, much as I loved them, I had not chosen my family, my street, my city or my country, and that I could not fathom what they thought I could do about being American. They all clapped and cheered, stating that they did not dislike me at all, just the current policies of my country. From there we developed some lasting, wonderful relationships.

Having made my final commitment in Joigny—and after serving

Washington, D.C.; Hope Rural School in Indiantown, Florida; St. Ignatius School in Grand Coteau, Louisiana; and Our Lady of Guadalupe School in Houston, Texas.
[32] *One Step Forward Towards Justice* [document] is available in the provincial archives in St. Louis.

briefly at our school in Cairo, Egypt, until the war of 1973 over the Sinai Peninsula broke out—I returned to the surprising news that I was to be the Headmistress of the Academy of the Sacred Heart in Bloomfield Hills, Michigan. I remained in that position for ten exciting years, and with that ministry came the great gift of working with Sister Kit Collins in many different capacities.

Little did I know then how significant had been the months before my start date as Headmistress, July 1, 1974. In January of that year, Sister Collins had written a paper articulating a rationale for a Network of Sacred Heart schools. She began with the following philosophical or directional paragraph:

> The chief strength, greatest asset and strongest bond of the Network of Sacred Heart schools derives from the common heritage and common purpose which these schools hold. It is this that gives the Network of schools both its *raison d'être* and its greatest possibility for effectiveness. From time to time expression is given to the Sacred Heart philosophy and goals as they apply to the contemporary world and its demands for strong, effective, religious and value-centered education.

She went on to quote from the previously mentioned key documents: the *General Chapter* of 1970, the *Objectives and Criteria for Sacred Heart Schools in North America* as articulated by the Heads at their meeting at Maryville during the 1971 Stuart Conference, and the document *One Step Forward Toward Justice*, in which Heads of School, at their meeting in March 1973, called each school to take one step forward toward justice within the coming year. Finally, her paper includes a listing of programmatic/personnel areas in which the Network was already functioning at that time, such as national and international student exchange programs; faculty exchange and program sharing; and planning for the 1974 Stuart Conference, to be held in July in Cleveland at John Carroll University.

In 1974, when I was named Headmistress at Bloomfield Hills, I began to know Sister Collins very well. Bloomfield Hills was one of the first Sacred Heart schools to have a local Board of Trustees. Because of the painful experience of closing the school across town in Grosse Pointe, the lay members of the Board insisted that we have a majority of RSCJ on our

Board. Sister Collins was one of those trustees and thus came to Bloomfield Hills five times per year with her high spirits and insightful contributions. She also worked closely with her "School Committee," which consisted of one Head from each of the five Provinces. During the 1974-75 school year, I replaced Sister Margaret Brown as the representative of the New York Province on the School Committee. Thus, I also met with Sister Collins several times per year at the newly formed national educational office in the Washington Province provincial house.

As we return with hindsight to these critically important years in the life of the Society of the Sacred Heart, we can see with clarity the various strands that contributed to the birth of the Network of Sacred Heart Schools and imposed upon them a certain amount of coherence. It seems to me that primary among those strands were the General Chapters of 1967 and 1970, thus underscoring the fundamental international identity of the Society and the fact that our schools desired to function within that internationality. In the words of Sister Concepción Camacho, the newly elected Superior General, at the close of the General Chapter of 1970:

> Only a contemplative study of events and persons can commit us to building a more human world, and make us feel how urgent is its call to us. This serious, prayerful attitude will unite us closely among ourselves and make us live today with renewed fidelity the spirit of our Constitutions.

These words express so very well the mission that the Network of Sacred Heart Schools has embraced during these many years since its birth—as well as anticipate the creation of the Goals and Criteria.

CHAPTER 4

Explorations of Governance

THE WINDHAM CONFERENCE AND
THE REFECTORY MODEL

The year 1974 was significant for the creation and birth of the Network of Sacred Heart Schools. Another important strand in the tapestry that we have come to know as the Network was a gathering from April 2 to 5, 1974, in Windham, New York. The Interprovincial Board asked Sisters Kit Collins, Judy Cagney, and Nance O'Neil to research and create possible future models of governance for the schools that would (1) enable the Provincials to exercise their authority for the living of the Society's mission in the schools, and (2) take advantage of lay involvement and expertise, where appropriate, in the governance of the schools.

At the time, having completed the program as a Sloan Fellow at M.I.T. (the first woman to do so), Sister O'Neil was serving as the finance officer for the New York Province. She was eventually named the first Provincial of the United States Province in 1982. Sister Cagney was to serve as President of Barat College in Lake Forest, Illinois, from 1975 to 1982, and would subsequently serve as the finance officer of the new United States Province. They invited David Ruhmkorff and Bruce Rogers of Management Design Incorporated (MDI) to join them. David and Bruce had already proved to be particularly insightful in consulting with administration teams in our schools across the country as we were forging our new vision of education. It is important to remember that the Windham Conference took place when we were midstream in the creation of the first Goals and Criteria of 1975 (the subject of our next chapter). We did not yet have a clear and finally approved articulation of our philosophy of education for the Network of Sacred Heart Schools.

From this gathering came a comprehensive paper entitled *The Refectory Model*. It describes both the highly centralized and uniform worldwide system of governance in the Society of the Sacred Heart before Vatican II, and the decentralized and confusing system of governance that had emerged after Vatican II. The following two quotations from the opening "Background" section of this sixty-five-page paper provide clear examples of the life that was lived before Vatican II:

> The arrangement of refectories around the world was determined in Rome.[33] The centralization of most aspects of our lives was nearly absolute. Decisions of any magnitude were made in Rome. Thus, Rome would give or withhold permission to put up or take down a wall between classrooms. The choice of orders of day was made in Rome: two choices, one beginning at 5:00 a.m., the other at 5:30 a.m. In what followed until 9:35 or 10:05 p.m. there were no choices. Even the Vicar was not at liberty to change that. There was a plan of studies for the schools, syllabi within the vicariate and even vicariate tests. The Motherhouse determined where the excess of income of any school would go.

The next quote directly addresses the nature of personal interactions:

> The normal silence at meals is indicative of the impersonality which marked most relationships. Two people could sit next to each other at every meal for a year—or even ten or twenty years—and they would not be expected to have talked [at a rare "talking meal"] of anything "personal" or of their families, or of politics. One was expected to speak about what was personal only with the Superior. Similar limitations on communications extended to the schools: Only the Mistress General (Headmistress) was to talk personally with the students, and only she or the Mistress of Studies spoke with

---

[33] Use of the word "Rome" in this quotation refers to the central government of the Society of the Sacred Heart. It does not refer to the Pope or other Vatican officials.

parents. Classroom teachers did not communicate with parents of their pupils.

The major portion of the rest of this paper describes seven possible governance structures for the Provincials to consider for adoption. Each was different, but all led to significant implications for the Provinces, and all implied questions as to whether the five-Province structure would continue as it had been.

The paper opens with a section of assumptions concerning the possible governance models and a section on the current status of school governance in each of the five Provinces. This section concludes with a paragraph entitled "compatibility" that proved to be very significant:

> Compatibility of the various forms of governance appears to be severely strained particularly if considered within an interprovincial context. This is not to say that any one form is superior to the others, but rather that if indeed the Society is to link its schools in some kind of national network, the task may shortly become exceedingly difficult, if not impossible. . . . In other words, where school governance is undergoing revision, those involved have no clear sense of parameters demanded by the Society, or what form of relationship to the Society is clearly acceptable (and hopefully effective). Were this to be worked out prior to a local Board's recommendations, hopes might be higher, confidence greater, and commitment stronger—and the apostolic work of the Society in the United States through its institutions, enhanced by a genuine national network.

In other words, the paper makes exceedingly clear the added challenge posed by the "interprovincial context" within which all of this change was to occur.

The development of alternative models of governance was accomplished in two steps: (1) the design of a model and (2) the identification of the implications within that model. These implications included the following areas: Society membership, leadership development, local school religious faculty, lay faculty, local school administration, constituency, sense of "birthright," Provincial structure (within an individual Province, within the whole), control, ownership, governance change potential, institutional change potential, finance, accountability to and for the Goals of the Society, present developing school governance, and staff functions.

THE SEVEN MODELS OF GOVERNANCE

The paper then goes on to introduce the seven models, noting that "serious consideration can be given to the compatibility of two or more models in combination." These models included (1) the National School Board Model; (2) the National School Board-Option Model; (3) the Franchise Model; (4) the Autonomy Model; (5) the Federation Model; (6) the Consortium Model; and (7) the Order Model.

The National School Board Model would involve an expansion of the IPB by religious and/or lay membership when the meeting concerned school matters that fell within the scope of such a Board. Membership on the Board could be regional in order to facilitate effective procedures for accountability to each of the five Provincials. Thus, the structure for school governance would not be identical with that for the Province membership. The School Board would consist of an expanded Interprovincial Board. The Board would establish policy regarding goals, planning, accountability, and evaluation, specifically in relation to the consonance of the schools' goals and operation with the Chapter Options, Society goals, etc.

The only difference between the previous model and **The National School Board Option Model** is that in the second the Board would be distinct in membership from the IPB. The IPB, however, would have the power to approve or to veto. The five Provincials would appoint this Board, consisting of lay and religious members.

In many ways, given the highly hierarchical character of the Society of the Sacred Heart up until Vatican II, one of the National Board models would have been most familiar to those already working in Sacred Heart schools.

In **The Franchise Model**, a "school franchise" would work in much the same way as any other franchise. That is, any school—through its Board of Trustees—could apply for a 'franchise' to be a Sacred Heart School. Operation under that franchise would involve acceptance of a commitment to a certain set of clearly stated goals and policies for Sacred Heart schools as well as strict accountability for their implementation.

In return, the Society would provide certain services (e.g. personnel, curriculum consultation, leadership, membership in the network). The IPB would grant (possibly by sale or lease) franchises to independent Boards of Trustees. This model allowed us to imagine an expansion of Sacred Heart education. In 1974, the concept of a franchise was to become a topic of lively conversation, both positive and negative, among the Heads of School and quickly became known as the McDonald's model.

The Autonomy Model is essentially one in which no governance by the Society would exist as such. Each school would set up its own independent Board of Trustees, which would purchase or otherwise assume the school property. Thus, there would be no binding relationship to the Society, although the Society could serve as a resource to any of the schools and influence them through its RSCJ members. Adoption and conformity to Society goals would be voluntary. Any school could seek to contract for Society services. There is no question that those in authority in each of the five Provinces who favored this model breathed a collective sigh of relief at the thought of having no responsibility for so many complex institutions.

The Federation Model was designed basically according to the governmental system of the United States. In this case, the rights and powers of a central government would be specified, and certain other rights and powers would be reserved to the local schools. The Legislative function of the whole would be exercised by a body composed of representatives from each of the local schools within the federation; the Judicial function (basically evaluative) would be carried out by the religious membership; and the Executive function would be reserved to the IPB. A constitution would be developed. It would include a statement of purpose or rationale; specified powers of the central government; specified powers that would be reserved to local schools; and provision for a system of checks and balances. Major goals and policies would be clearly established by the IPB. This model produced much conversation and was hailed as a structure that promoted the vision and goal of the network's becoming a community of persons, much like a family, of those embracing the Sacred Heart philosophy.

In **The Consortium Model,** an association of schools would be established by agreement, involving a common statement of philosophy or purpose and certain general policies. There would be no formal means of accountability, either among the schools themselves, or between the schools and the Society. In this case, neither the Provinces nor the IPB would have any binding responsibility toward the schools, and vice-versa. Schools would be bound together in the Spirit. Together, as a consortium, they would agree to a statement of philosophy. Schools would operate autonomously, implementing in their own ways the intent of the philosophical statement. Accountability would not be structurally defined; rather it would be accomplished through moral suasion. The IPB and Provincial governments would have no governing responsibility toward the schools. I never heard any enthusiasm for this Consortium model.

Finally, **The Order Model** provided for up-and-down communication between the Society of the Sacred Heart and the schools. The National Staff would be responsible for the dissemination of information and maintenance of records, and for making each school aware of its strengths and challenges by visitations. An Education Committee would be formed, consisting of teachers, trustees, heads and other school administrators, people from our colleges and from apostolates[34] other than our schools, and even people not associated with any school. An Executive Committee and officers would be elected by the Education Committee annually. All schools would be guided by the Education Committee in their value position and would report to it. Common arrangements for public relations, fund raising, recruitment and curriculum development would be made by the Education Committee and implemented by the national staff, who would maintain a resource file of people and their expertise. In this model, all Sacred Heart schools would theoretically have a common value system, and control of the Network would be shared by teachers, trustees and administrators—religious and lay.

The concluding remarks of the papers submitted to the IPB from the Windham Conference indicate significant problems and concerns that could arise in the future for the Society and its schools in the United States. First, they speak of Religious-lay collaboration within both the Church and the Society, pointing out the reality that serious Religious-lay

---

[34] "Apostolate" is a term derived from the word "apostle." It refers to a ministry or work undertaken with a sense of mission. Other examples undertaken by RSCJ include spiritual direction, hospital work, and direct service with the poor and marginalized.

collaboration is not only necessary, but valued. They state that what needs to be examined with great care (and ultimately determined in some way) is at what levels such collaboration is in fact appropriate, desirable, and effective. In other words, the conclusion asks: Is there a distinction to be made between the functions of *interpretation* (as related to the spirit of the Society) and *implementation* (the meaning of decisions within a given context)?

Next, they note issues of membership because of the manner in which apostolates had developed in the post-1967 era. Some sense of "dis-membering" had accompanied the professionalization of administrative practices in the schools and the diversification of apostolic works. There seemed, in short, to be ambiguity about exactly *what* constituted membership in the Society. The Windham participants raised two key questions about membership: (1) Is there a sense in which lay collaborators have some kind of membership in the Society? and (2) What constitutes membership among the Religious of the Society?

They then speak of difficulties concerning financial responsibility and decision-making. For example, to ask fiscal responsibility of a local Board while reserving the right of decision-making to a Provincial or Interprovincial group could present serious difficulties. In fact, it is remarkable that they so ably predicted issues and concerns that Network schools and the Network as a whole were to encounter in the years to come.

They state, too, that clarification of governance structures may in itself generate resistance because of the potential for a perceived loss of power on the part of those most closely involved at the local level. They note that the layers involved in the governing structure of the Society seemed to generate multiple modes of accountability, a situation that was further compounded by adding the layers of local and/or provincial boards. It would be imperative to clarify the function of each layer.

Leadership training is cited as an area of increasingly critical concern. A brief review of the Religious in the United States had indicated that a significant number of Religious possessed both the talent for and the interest in assuming positions of institutional leadership. The spotting and subsequent training (at the national level) of such administrative talent would be the most desirable approach.

They conclude that a successful resolution of the school governance question at the national level would depend to a great extent on the collaborative effort of the school heads and the IPB. They ask the question: Might it be possible, and most appropriate, for the Heads of School to serve as a recommending body, along with the Provincial Teams and any others determined by the IPB? It was clear that governance would become a major topic on the agenda of the Heads meeting in 1974.

Finally, those gathered in Windham clearly realized that their study contained a number of implications for re-organization of the Society of the Sacred Heart's five-province structure. They concluded by raising the following very significant and perceptive questions:

> Would it be advantageous to organize the institutions nationally and the membership locally?
>
> How much overlap and duplication of work is there among those in Provincial Staff positions—education, finance, personnel, formation?
>
> Could the development and placement of personnel be not only more efficient but more effective if it were done nationally rather than provincially or interprovincially?
>
> What is the primary responsibility of provincial government? Is it institutional and apostolic leadership? spiritual leadership? trouble shooting? personnel placement?
>
> Is there a way of developing spiritual leadership at the community level in such a way as to free the Provincial and her team to spend their time and energy on chosen priorities?
>
> What kind of organization would be best suited to the development of an apostolic consciousness that is both national and worldwide? What potential have the institutions in this regard?

The Windham Conference concluded with the recommendation to the IPB that the foregoing governance models should be discussed at the Heads meeting to take place at the next Stuart Conference. This conference would be held in the summer of 1974 at John Carroll University in Cleveland.

THE 1974 STUART CONFERENCE

Within this context, on July 1, 1974, I began what was to be my ten-year tenure as Headmistress of the Academy of the Sacred Heart in Bloomfield Hills, Michigan. As stated previously, in 1973 Sister Collins had appointed a School Committee consisting of one Head of School from each of the five Provinces to work with her.[35] They had already begun the work of developing the Goals and Criteria of 1975, focusing on the information gathered from all the communities of Religious of the Sacred Heart in February of 1972, plus input from the Heads of School at the 1971 Stuart Conference and the One Step Forward Toward Justice gathering in March of 1973. Now the heads' agenda of 1974 was to give them the opportunity to discuss and endorse one or more of the government systems developed at the Windham meeting.

Sister Collins opened the 1974 Stuart Conference with a speech that became a cornerstone in the development of our Network of Sacred Heart Schools. Pointing clearly towards the Goals and Criteria she said:

> We are all aware, some perhaps more than others, of the struggle of these past few years to clarify, identify, to articulate what it really means to be a Sacred Heart School, and what Sacred Heart education really means. That, I believe, is a life-long struggle, and I hope it will never be otherwise. But, I think there are some things we can look to for reflection, and hopefully for enlightenment. The first of those, and perhaps the most obvious, is that which we draw from – the history and the tradition of Sacred Heart schools, best expressed perhaps in what we have called the *Plan of Studies*—which is really an incredible document—which was frequently and seriously updated from 1805 until 1958 when the title was significantly changed to *Spirit and Plan of Studies*.

Her remarks were filled with language and phrasing that have become central to Sacred Heart education in the subsequent decades. Synthesizing the wisdom of previous Sacred Heart educators with the excitement and

---

[35] The first committee included Sisters Helen Condon, Shirley Connolly, Judy Garson, Carol Purtle, and Nancy Salisbury.

change of post-Vatican II Catholicism, she articulated a philosophy of education whose phrasing is a clear harbinger of the first iteration of the Goals and Criteria:

> We find there (in the *Spirit and Plan of Studies*) a clear emphasis, and we all know this, I think, on the education of the whole child. We find insistence on strong intellectual formation, firm moral development, active social concern, deep respect for individual uniqueness, a caring use of knowledge in the service of others, insistence on religious teaching, and more importantly, on religion itself as inseparable from life . . . in the last analysis, we educate by who we are, and by the structures and the processes we establish for learning.

She made further reference to the notion of justice and the imperative of educating students to go out into the world and work for the "right use of power":

> This is all by way of saying that the meaning of Sacred Heart education, and of being Sacred Heart educators, is related directly, traditionally, historically, symbolically, theologically and etymologically to the demand of justice, to the call for integrity, to the right use of power so badly needed today.

Towards the end of the speech Sister Collins, referencing the sad state of contemporary American politics,[36] called out the very best in us:

> This means that in the school, the student can be socialized to a lack of integrity, to injustice and to the misuse of power—and that (in the age of Watergate) is a very frightening thing. But it can also mean that in the school the student can be educated to integrity, to justice as a way of life, and to the pure use of power. And that is awesome, but I think it is tremendously exciting.

After raising an array of questions that made us examine the structures in our schools and the quality of life for our students, Sister Collins closed with a favorite quotation of hers from Tennyson's "Ulysses":

---

[36] This was the era of the Watergate scandal.

> Come, my friends
> 'Tis not too late to seek a newer world.
> Push off, and sitting well in order smite
> The sounding furrows; for my purpose holds
> To sail beyond the sunset, and the baths
> Of all the Western stars, until I die.
> . . .
> Though much is taken much abides; and though
> We are not now that strength which in old days
> Moved earth and heaven; that which we are, we are,
> One equal temper of heroic hearts,
> Made weak by time and fate, but strong in will
> To strive, to seek, to find, and not to yield.

With these inspiring words, our National Coordinator for Sacred Heart Education launched the 1974 Stuart Conference. The contrast between the agenda for the 1969 Stuart Conference and the conference of 1974 is remarkable and instructive. In 1969 the agenda was printed back and front on an 8 ½ by 11 piece of paper. In 1974, the agenda had to be printed in a multi-page booklet. Again, workshops and group meetings not only provided educational input and meaningful discussions, but also provided a myriad of community-building experiences for Sacred Heart educators.

I remember well the Heads of School meeting that followed the 1974 Stuart Conference. This was my first Heads of School meeting, and Sister Collins and her school committee required hard work and much concentration from us. We considered each of the seven governance models developed at Windham in terms of the long list of possible implications that had also been developed at Windham.

None of the models was endorsed in its entirety by the Heads of School, but it was clearly becoming increasingly important to them to discuss in ever greater detail the pros and cons of moving toward one rather than five Provinces in this country. Following the Heads' meeting, Sister Collins sent a memo to the Provincials saying: "When the School Committee and group leaders met to 'wrap up' objective two (governance models) of the Heads of School meeting in Cleveland, it was suggested by the entire group that the Provincials be asked to suspend any major changes in school governance until we reach greater clarity on the issue (which shouldn't take too long)."

Eventually the IPB adopted a model of governance that included local Boards of Trustees and a national system of accountability to the Society for the mission of the Society of the Sacred Heart. This system was originally called the National Commission on Goals and now, in 2017, the Sacred Heart Commission on Goals. In fact, adoption of independent Boards of Trustees happened slowly across the country from 1975 to 1995. In many instances possible board members stated that they were happy to provide their thinking and expertise in areas such as finance, buildings and grounds, legal issues, fund-raising and the like. But it was imperative that the RSCJ themselves first articulate their philosophy of education, their mission.

CHAPTER 5

The Goals and Criteria

RESTRUCTURING

At this point, countless conversations and meetings were happening in each of the five Provinces and among the many RSCJ who realized that the future of the Society of the Sacred Heart in the United States rested in their hands. A letter dated May 1972 from Sister Beatrice Brennan to her Provincial, Sister Mavie Coakley, seems to express the thinking of some RSCJ in this tumultuous period. Sister Brennan had held many positions of leadership in the New York Province and at this time was the Headmistress of the Academy of the Sacred Heart in Bloomfield Hills, Michigan.

She begins by expressing eloquently her case for creating a network of Sacred Heart schools. After dismissing a perceived concern that such a move would constitute a negative reaction toward those choosing "other apostolates," she goes on to assert that such a network would be the single way in which the RSCJ might maintain a significant communitarian ministry. In the language of the 1970s, such group apostolates represented a "corporate thrust," or common apostolic impact, for religious congregations. The following quotation from Sister Brennan states her case for a network of schools very well:

> There seems to be an underlying assumption that if we are all in this thing together as RSCJ we are exercising a "corporate thrust." I cannot agree with this assumption, except in those

places where we own and control the institutions within which RSCJ are working. In all other instances, we exercise either an individual influence or a communal influence as a group of individuals. In the future, this may be the only way we choose to serve as RSCJ in education. Meanwhile, we have one alternative we still can explore as a corporate body: the network of schools which are still ours to direct, and which could do something together that they cannot do as individual schools.

She then articulates the reality that the seven remaining Sacred Heart colleges[37] still offered varying degrees of possibility for a corporate thrust, but that legal questions regarding their governance and control would seem too complex to allow for much, if any, official collaboration among them. This seemed to her, and to many others, even more true of those other institutions within which RSCJ were working in related apostolates. She goes on to expostulate that what these religious (as well as those working in the colleges) needed was a sense that they were indeed carrying out the Society's educational mission. But—typical of this period's shift from hierarchical to grass roots thinking—she believed that they themselves would have to sense these needs before any kind of effective structures could be developed for them. Sister Brennan also suggested that a proposed "Interprovincial Coordinator" write to each RSCJ in higher education and in related apostolates during 1972-1973, and take their replies as an indication of what kinds of structures needed to be set up.

While other IPB staff members would focus on the colleges and other apostolates, Sister Brennan was clearing the way for the creation of a staff position whose role would be to focus exclusively on the Network of Sacred Heart Schools. She foresaw that the position would require an enormous commitment and the complete attention of whoever stepped into it: "For her to take on anything else would, I fear, mean that nothing would be

---

[37] These were Newton, Lone Mountain, Duchesne, Barat, Manhattanville, Maryville, and San Diego College for Women. Ultimately, Newton College of the Sacred Heart became part of Boston College, Lone Mountain College became part of the University of San Francisco, Duchesne College in Omaha and Barat College in Lake Forest subsequently closed, Manhattanville College and Maryville College both became secular colleges, and San Diego College for Women became part of the University of San Diego.

done well." She also suggested with her typical clear thinking that instead of "Apostolic Coordinator," she might be called "Coordinator of Schools" or something that would clearly express the limits of her function. Such a job description would obviously have to be clearly defined, and she suggested that the current school Principals be involved in the writing of it.

In the same letter, and doubtless in consultation with many thoughtful RSCJ, Sister Brennan proposed the first Network Coordinator's job description. This person's role and responsibilities would include the following:

1. To find out by personal observation and by consultation with key people at the provincial and local levels, just what is noteworthy about the education now going on in each school. This would probably take at least a year to complete.

2. To find out how other networks of schools operate, e.g. The Friends schools, the Jesuits, etc.

3. To work closely with those in leadership roles in the schools and in the Provinces in their own long-range planning, to see in what ways these plans could be fitting into a larger national picture, e.g. the possibility of developing one super-fine teacher training center at one of them, which might have close ties with a neighboring university.

4. To bring small groups of people together to accomplish some clearly defined task for the schools as the need arises.

5. To go in search of just the right consultant to help the schools get a common project off the ground, or to show a group working on a common task how this kind of thing has been tackled successfully by others in the field.

6. To represent the Sacred Heart schools as a group with national organizations, e.g. NAIS, etc.

7. To do none of these things unless the need seems to emerge from the local level, but to be sensitive to needs even before they have been articulated by people too busy doing to have time for talking or dreaming.

8. To encourage by her own enthusiasm the faith of those working in the schools in the value of what they are doing and the possibilities for growth.

9. To keep in close touch with the motherhouse in Rome so that real possibilities for international linkages, which they may have uncovered in their travels, may become realities.

10. To keep in touch with AASH (Associated Alumnae/i of the Sacred Heart) officers so that their present keen interest in Sacred Heart education, especially in the student exchange project, may be fostered and developed.

11. To do whatever else seems useful in forming the schools into a vital network, a kind of federation, which takes nothing from the autonomy of the individual school, but enhances it by putting at its disposal the richness available in others of its kind.

Sister Brennan went on to say what so many others were thinking at the time: "This is a tall order, obviously. I suggest that we are fortunate to have someone not only eminently talented for this kind of task but also now doing it for the Washington Province: Sister Kit Collins." She asked that the Washington Province consider releasing Sister Collins from her current responsibilities in order that she might perform the same service for the entire country. Rather than dropping her current responsibilities, however, she would be allowed to relinquish some of the details to an assistant in order to begin doing groundwork for all five Provinces.

In September of 1972, the Interprovincial Board met to discuss the proposed restructuring of the Board. At this stage, the IPB undertook to discuss and come to some agreement upon many different topics, only some of which involved the schools. Examples of these topics included: the selection of a novice director; possible combined investments; planning for an international meeting with all the Provincials in Latin America; a request from Rome for RSCJ to move to Korea, at least for a short period of time; a request that some RSCJ be asked to research and study all the Bishops' statements on justice; the development of policies for RSCJ, some by Province and some for the whole country; and the appointment of an ad hoc committee to study the re-structuring of the five Provinces. The Provincials at this time were Sisters Elizabeth Cavanagh, Mavie Coakley, Jean Ford, Agnes Lahey from Canada, Beatrice Mardel, and Margaret Mary Miller. Staff to the IPB included Sisters Judy Cagney, Kit Collins, Ann Conroy, Rosemary Dewey, Rita Karam and Nance O'Neil.

In October of 1972 Sister Jean Ford, then the Provincial of the Washington Province and Chair of the IPB, sent a memo to all the Principals and Directors of Education in the five Provinces. In many ways, it was a culmination of all the conversations of many years. Her clear thinking and good communication skills were critically important during this period of 1967–1972, when so much change could have resulted in chaos rather than the solid, well-defined structures that resulted in our Network of Sacred Heart Schools. Sister Ford was eventually to serve on the first national Provincial Team under the leadership of Sister Nance O'Neil beginning in 1982; she later served on the Central Team in Rome.

Highlights of her October 1972 memo included the landmark decision to appoint Sister Collins to the IPB staff as Coordinator of Schools. She went on to say that it was felt by many that Sister Collins, whose experience was now enriched by her recent experience working with multiple schools, would most ably discharge this responsibility. She explained that Sister Collins could continue projects just undertaken in both the Washington and New York Provinces as well as suggest programs that could be expanded on a national basis. She had the unique experience at that time of having worked across geographic and provincial boundaries. Sister Collins would remain for now Director of Education for the Washington Province and continue to be based at the Washington Province Provincial House in Newton, Massachusetts. But in this new position, she would also begin to work—at their request—with schools all over the United States.

It is important to understand that Sister Collins brought broad vision, lively intelligence and a wonderful sense of humor to this new position. She saw clearly what so many who came before and after her, including St. Madeleine Sophie Barat, had seen: that education was critical to any attempt to improve a world so very much in need of it. This serious need for excellent education seemed to be particularly apparent in the late 1960s and early 1970s. Sister Collins was a woman of her times and saw the great need for a major step toward justice and respect for all persons. Similarly, Madeleine Sophie Barat was a woman of her times and believed in education, especially of women, as the means toward positive social and spiritual change. Sister Collins also shared Sophie's understanding that at a given historical moment, structures need to change.[38]

Sister Collins' job description in this initial stage was to include the creation of a School Committee composed of one Head of School from each Province. It was felt that a committee consisting of all Heads of School would be "too unwieldy," but that a committee of five heads or principals in addition to Sister Collins would provide a balanced view from around the United States. This structure had worked well for the finance and personnel committees of the IPB.

The job description made it abundantly clear that the IPB also wanted Sister Collins to continue to work with the Stuart Committee in organizing Stuart Conferences. The Provincials obviously recognized the importance of these large, spirit-filled gatherings and wanted to communicate that the creation of the School Committee did not in any way eliminate the need for the Stuart Committee. Distinct from the School Committee, which would be composed of administrators, the Stuart Committee would continue to be composed of creative, cutting-edge educators drawn from a variety of Sacred Heart Schools.

Her job description would also include facilitating communication between the Interprovincial Board and the Provincial Education Directors; and facilitating communication between the IPB and the Heads of School, especially with regard to any issues before the Board that would affect education in our schools. It should be noted that for some time, each Province had had a Director of Education who supervised the workings of each school in her Province. Each director performed her duties in a unique way, depending on the needs of her Province and her particular educational gifts. Some were providing very creative leadership while others were more prescriptive in their approach.

Sister Collins would also be asked to provide a variety of services to faculties, especially in those areas in which inter-school planning or programming might be involved. An early example of such national

---

[38] During her lifetime, Sophie undertook two significant restructurings of the Society. One (beginning in 1839 and not resolved until 1842) involved the location of the motherhouse and the precise nature of the relationship between and among the Society, the Vatican, and the French bishops. The second, in 1851, involved (among other things) a restructuring of the Society into separate Vicariates.

projects was the student exchange program, whereby a student from one school would study at another and be hosted by a local Sacred Heart family. There was lively interest in such exchanges all across the country, but exchanges did not actually take place until the Network was a reality.

An important administrative function of the Network Coordinator would also be the calling of an annual meeting of the Heads of School. It was hoped that such meetings would take place in conjunction with one of the IPB meetings. Sister Collins would also be responsible for initiating, through the Stuart Committee, the planning for the biennial Stuart Conference. And finally, as the schools moved from the familiar model of relating to one of the five Provincials to relating to the Network Coordinator, it was important that communication be provided through some sort of bulletin that her office would publish. In addition to all of this, schools could request other kinds of educational services from the Network Coordinator on an ad hoc basis.

And so, in the 1972-73 school year, Sister Collins embraced her new, very complex job and moved forward with her vision of building a community of Sacred Heart students and educators that stretched north and south, east and west in the United States.

THE GOALS AND CRITERIA OF SACRED HEART EDUCATION

By this time, it was very apparent, for the many reasons outlined previously, that the Society had to articulate clearly our philosophy of education and find a way to monitor its implementation in each school. This articulation became the critical focus of the work of the School Committee from 1973 until 1975. The many previous gatherings—from the Heads meeting at the 1971 Stuart Conference at Maryville to the One Step Forward meeting of the 1973 Heads of School in Washington, D.C.—as well as the contributions of all the RSCJ in the United States to the document of February of 1972, had generated list after list of possible descriptions of the fundamental components of Sacred Heart education. Now it was time for Sister Collins and her School Committee to pull all of these documents into a coherent statement of the essentials of Sacred Heart education in the late twentieth century.

Membership on the School Committee rotated among the Heads of School in each of the five Provinces. Thus, many different Heads played a part in creating the Goals and Criteria of 1975. The first committee from 1973 to 1974 included Sisters Helen Condon from the Chicago Province; Shirley Connolly of the California Province; Judy Garson, a member of the New York Province but representing the Washington Province, where she was Head of School in Princeton, New Jersey; Carol Purtle from the Southern Province; and Nancy Salisbury from the New York Province. In 1974, the composition of the committee changed to include Heads of School George Bryan from the Chicago Province and William Gallop from the Southern Province, Sisters Margaret Brown from the New York Province, Sister Joan McKenna from the California Province and Sister Judy Garson from the Washington Province. In 1975, membership on the committee shifted again when Sister Marie-Louise Flick from the California Province and I from the New York Province replaced Sisters Joan McKenna and Margaret Brown.

My most vivid personal memory of those 1975 meetings includes the day when Sister Judy Garson quietly left for another room. In what seemed to be a very short time she returned having written the irreplaceable Preamble to the Goals and Criteria, a statement that has become, word for word, an unchanging component of this central document of Sacred Heart education. No matter how many times we have updated the Goals and Criteria over the past forty years, this important expression of our philosophical heritage as Sacred Heart educators has remained unchanged.

In 2015, I contacted Sister Judy Garson and Sister Marie Louise Flick for their memories of those days. It is important once again to remember that we had received input from every community in the country, as well as from every faculty and staff member. In the words of Sister Garson, "We were *drowning* in input."

Sister Garson remembers the early realization that the Goals would be a list, stating the essentials very simply as so many people had requested. With her typical clear thinking, however, Sister Garson saw that it would be critical to include Criteria under each Goal—Criteria that would put teeth into the statement. She saw even then that measurement, evaluation, and course corrections would be essential for the schools to be held accountable. With hindsight, we can now see clearly how critically important these Criteria have become.

Sister Garson's memory of writing the Preamble to the Goals and Criteria includes, too, the sense of being overwhelmed with the amount of input there was to peruse. She said: "So I was scribbling away, and suddenly I saw the essentials pretty clearly. You know that writing well in a group is all but impossible, so I said that if they'd trust me to put things down on paper I would pad off and do that for a while. *Voilà!* It seemed to work. The group was wonderful, of course . . . already a mix of RSCJ and laypeople who 'got it.'"

Sister Flick, too, remembers the mounds of material we had to sift through, all of it representing participation from so many people across the country. In addition to the voices of school leadership teams and individuals working in the schools, the material included the voices of all RSCJ who had participated in the discussions held at Provincial assemblies. She also remembers trying to incorporate the thinking of the Plan of Studies. As stated previously, this document, which had been written in St. Madeleine Sophie's day and revised several times since then (most recently in 1958), did not mesh easily with the new articulation of our educational vision. Nevertheless, Sister Flick continues, "This did not mean that we rejected such an important, influential work. The challenge, rather, was to keep its spirit alive in a modern way as our RSCJ sisters had done in the past."

Sister Flick also remembers important conversations at the School Committee meetings about our schools and the kinds of students we were educating at the time. As was true for several schools in the United States, Forest Ridge, our Sacred Heart school in Seattle where Sister Flick was in a leadership position, numbered only one third of its student body as Roman Catholic. "The rest were from various Christian denominations, and many were from Asian families of Buddhist or Hindu practices," she explains. "This colored how we developed religious studies and encouraged deeper conversations about 'lived faith' and the tradition of the Sacred Heart of Jesus. We were going through a period of time where the Devotion of the Sacred Heart was being replaced with language that came out of Vatican II theologians like Karl Rahner."[39]

---

[39] Karl Rahner, S.J., 1904-1984, was a prolific theologian whose work influenced the Second Vatican Council. The basis of his work is that all human beings have a latent

In fact, by the time the first version of the Goals and Criteria of Sacred Heart Education was published in April of 1975, two of the Criteria under the first Goal (then worded "Schools of the Sacred Heart commit to educating to a faith which is relevant in a secularized world") did specifically reference the name of Jesus: the first, "The school recognizes its life force in the love of Jesus Christ by supporting in concrete ways the value of reflection and of prayer"; and the sixth, "The school presents itself to the wider community as a Christ-centered institution within the evolving tradition of the Church." But discussions around this first Goal were in many respects fraught and reflected the larger debate going on within the Catholic Church at the time.

Sister Flick recalls that discussions around the second Goal, "Schools of the Sacred Heart commit to educating to a deep respect for intellectual values," were relatively easy. "I remember sailing through that topic and easily spouting ideas for Criteria. For all of us, strong intellectual formation was essential to the schools."

However, conversations and decisions about what to include in Goal Three ("Schools of the Sacred Heart commit to educating to a social awareness that impels to action") were more challenging. This was not the rhetoric of the day in St. Madeleine Sophie's nineteenth century, nor was it part of the usual conversation within the Roman Catholic Church until Vatican II.[40] Eventually it became clear to the members of the School Committee that there was a need for two separate Goals—one concerning building internal community in daily life and one concerning an outward thrust into the wider community. Sister Flick states that wording for Goal Three really came out of Stone Ridge, our Sacred Heart School in Bethesda, Maryland, which dared to devote a whole day of school each week to sending the students out into the community, having them reflect on their experiences upon their return, and taking them beyond

---

experience of God. It is only because of this that recognizing a distinctively special revelation is possible and can occur through a variety of faith traditions. His theology not only influenced the Second Vatican Council, but was also groundbreaking for the development of what is generally seen as the modern understanding of Catholicism.

[40] Exception should be made for Pope Leo XIII's 1891 encyclical on social justice (*Rerum novarum*) and two or three other encyclicals that followed from it before the opening of Vatican II.

the perimeters of their own worlds. "It was very impressive to me," Sister Flick commented.

As the committee worked to separate out the fourth Goal, "Schools of the Sacred Heart commit to educating to the building of community as a Christian value," the Criteria at first seemed relatively weak in contrast to those under the social awareness Goal. However, we have seen over the years that the strength of this Goal lies in the word *building*. It might seem simple to "have community," but *building* community in our homes and work places can be very challenging indeed, especially given the overwhelming emphasis on individualism in our culture. In a sense, this community Goal is the building block that underpins and enables social justice to happen at all.

The fifth and last Goal states, "Schools of the Sacred Heart commit to educating to personal growth in an atmosphere of wise freedom." It is interesting for those of us from different parts of the United States to note that the wording of the fifth and last Goal came directly from a lengthy discussion during the California Provincial Assembly. Sister Flick shares that the language itself was articulated by Sisters Marilyn McMorrow, Trudy Patch and Sally Furay. "I've always felt a bit proud that our province brought this to the table for discussion. Some thought that 'wise freedom' was redundant but in the end we kept it because of the issue of a certain 'license' in free behavior that can be particularly destructive for young people."

Cumbersome as it was to sort through so much input, the process we used enabled so many to find their contributions in the final document of the Goals and Criteria.

In April of 1975, the IPB met with the School Committee, and after some modification, approved the Goals and Criteria for Sacred Heart Schools in the United States, as well as a mode of evaluation to be implemented in a "pilot year" during the 1975-1976 academic year. Sister Flick remembers the moment when she first presented this new articulation of the Sacred Heart philosophy of education to an open meeting for parents and alumnae. When she introduced the Goals and Criteria, she saw the delight on the faces of loyal alums and faithful parents and felt "we had hit a home run."

It was established that in this first year, every school would go through a process of evaluation. Each school would design and implement its own process, and the evaluation visits would be coordinated and overseen within each of the five Provinces, which would send a team to their respective schools. At the end of the year, a major review of this evaluative system would take place in order to move forward to the IPB recommendations for its improvement. As events unrolled, each Province conducted the evaluations in a very different way, and the conclusion after this first year was that the process should become national rather than provincial in nature so that there would be consistency from one part of the country to another.

In an undated document from that era, written in the thorough manner that was characteristic of the leadership of Sister Collins, we find a listing of assumptions regarding the use of the final document of the Goals and Criteria. Each Head of School was asked to indicate her degree of agreement or disagreement with each of the assumptions. I include them here because, again, the work of the mid-1970s was to prove so significant for us in the following years. The assumptions we were asked to consider were the following:

1. That the primary responsibility of those who govern the school is to oversee effective implementation of these Goals and Criteria.
2. That this document will be used in hiring new faculty.
3. That this document will act as an evaluative tool.
4. That acceptance of these Goals and Criteria determines a school's belonging to the Sacred Heart Network.
5. That this document will be given to applicants who wish to attend the school.
6. That this is an evolving document based on evaluation.
7. That this document should be as brief, simple and well written as possible.
8. That each school will develop its own objectives in light of this document.
9. That this document will spark inter-provinciality and unity.
10. That this document will generate a renewed sense of hope and mission.

11. That this document will be an identifying instrument for determining whether a school is a Sacred Heart school.

12. That this document will require effective implementation and be a condition for remaining a member of the Sacred Heart Network.

13. That this document will be used by those who assume responsibility for managing the school.

One way or another each of these assumptions has proven to be significant.

We have only grown in our understanding that values left unarticulated are easily lost—and that those values we articulate must be *lived,* if we truly expect to communicate them to the students in our care and share them with our fellow educators. How many times have we as Sacred Heart educators proclaimed that one of the great gifts of the Goals and Criteria as we have lived them now for forty years is that we can never check them off as "finished"? There is always a next, best step that we can take with each Goal and Criterion in our institutions—and in our own lives.

Two quotations from those days stand out for me, first the frequently cited words of Walter Wink, a professor at Union Theological Seminary in New York:

> History belongs to the intercessors who believe the future into being. This is not simply a religious statement. The future belongs to whoever can envision in the manifold of its possibilities a new inevitability. That is the politics of hope. Hope envisions its future and then acts as if that future is irresistible, thus helping to create the reality for which it longs. The future is not closed, though there are fields of forces whose interactions are predictable. But how they will interact is not. Even a small number of people, totally committed to the new inevitability on which they have fixed their imaginations, can decisively affect the shape the future takes.[41]

---

[41] Walter Wink, 1935-2012, was an American Biblical scholar, theologian and activist, who was an important figure in progressive Christianity. He spent much of his career teaching at Auburn Theological Seminary in New York. Sister Collins frequently cited this quotation to underscore the importance of the Network of Sacred Heart Schools.

The second quotation is from Concepción Camacho, RSCJ, Superior General of the Society of the Sacred Heart during the challenging years of change from 1970 to 1982:

> Our education, our formation must not be artificial but deeply serious if we are to live our task of contemplation and struggle in today's world. We talk a great deal about presence, but being there is not everything. We must grow interiorly if we are to be qualified to be present in any setting. We must make ourselves whole, develop our intelligence, our will, our power of feeling, for all this is part of our charism.[42]

The Goals and Criteria have become more than a philosophy of education. Rather they have come to describe a philosophy of life for thousands of individuals and families.

---

[42] Talk delivered to Assembly of Provincials on March 14, 1975.

PART II

THE FIRST TWENTY-FIVE YEARS

CHAPTER 6

The Network Directed by Sister Kit Collins 1972–1984

This will lead us to commit the Society further to its apostolic mission. As Religious of the Sacred Heart, how can we, both by our life and by our work, convey to the world the message of the freely given love of God, which is revealed in His Son? The task demands a courageous habit of listening, testing, searching; a broad vision of the world and of what is at stake in the Kingdom, which demands that we be detached, self-sacrificing, at the disposal of others.

~ Mother Maria Josefa Bultó, Superior General[43]

With the spirit of courage and broad vision suggested by Mother Bultó's words, Sister Collins, soon to be empowered by the creation of the Goals and Criteria, began to lead the Network of Sacred Heart Schools in the United States. As discussed earlier, Sister Collins—prior to the final articulation of the Goals and Criteria in 1975—had led the Heads of School in the One Step Forward to Justice meeting in 1973; taken part in the Windham Conference in 1974; and worked with the Stuart Committee to plan the Stuart Conference of 1974. But of foremost importance was

---

[43] Opening Session of the 1970 General Chapter.

her intuition that none of these strands could come together in forming a network of schools without a clear articulation of the philosophy of Sacred Heart education for this moment in history. This, of course, was the primary task of the School Committee from 1973 to 1975, as we focused our attention on input from every community and every faculty and staff member in the United States Sacred Heart schools.

COMMISSION ON GOALS

Once the Goals and Criteria were approved by the five Provincials in 1975, it was Sister Collins' spirited leadership that enabled the formation of the National Commission on Goals. To review, this commission had the task of creating a process whereby each school could give evidence to the Provincial and her team that it was indeed responsibly living the mission of the Society.

From the beginning, it was clear that this mission would be lived differently in the diverse cities and regions of the United States. Of great help to us was Thomas Groome of Boston College, who acted as our consultant and introduced us to the method known as Shared Praxis. We created a timeline wherein four or five schools were visited each year on a five-year cycle. Each October, a national meeting introduced those who would visit the schools to the Shared Praxis method and the protocols so important to a school visit. Over the many years since then the methodology has evolved, but always the schools have been held accountable for living the mission of the Goals and Criteria and articulating their next steps for doing so on a regular basis.

In October of 1979, at the Commission on Goals training session, Sister Collins' presentation entitled *Story/Vision* included themes that were consistent throughout her years as Director of the Network:

> I'd like to think not of membership as in a club, but membership as in a body, an image deeply rooted in the tradition of the Church and Scripture. . . . So the Sacred Heart Network is not only a network of schools but, much more importantly, a network of people, and as such, we are bound together by a past, a heritage that is strong and beautiful and extends in time. . . . We are also bound together by hope in the future, . . .

and it's those two things, our memory and our vision, our story and our vision, that always keep us moving from who and what we have been to what we want to become. It's important to stay in touch with our past, but not to stay in it; not stay tied in our past in the sense of nostalgia because to stay tied to the past is to disbelieve in the future and that's despair. It's also important to locate ourselves in a larger framework in the present where our memory and our vision come together, a larger framework in the present. . . . So I'd now like to focus on the Goals and Criteria.

Over and over again, Sister Collins led us back to the Goals and Criteria and the wide-ranging and healthy philosophy of education, of life, that they represent. She was also clearly committed to calling us to integrate this vision with the times in which we lived. Sacred Heart education had been rooted successfully in cultures on every major continent because it combined the ability to touch its participants at their deepest core of meaning while integrating that vision with the events of our evolving world.

NETWORK MEETINGS AND STUDENT LEADERSHIP CONFERENCES

Large Stuart Conferences gave way to smaller meetings, usually gatherings of like ministries to share best practices, to discuss how to implement the Goals and Criteria in one's particular area of school life, and to hear new calls in Sacred Heart education. Sister Collins' intent in these meetings was to build relationships and friendships among Sacred Heart educators and to foster ownership of the Goals and Criteria and the Network of Sacred Heart Schools. Such meetings were held for people holding similar job descriptions within the schools, such as Heads of School, division heads, business managers, development directors, campus ministers, and subject area teachers.

Student Leadership conferences were also initiated. The goal of these conferences was to provide training for student leaders at the national level. In this way, again, relationships and friendships were fostered so that these student leaders could begin to understand themselves and their role as part of a larger network and live out their mission across the United States. Student comments following the 1983 leadership conference reflected the success of such gatherings. Dee Dawson, President of the Student Council at Duchesne in Houston, said, "I gained a better understanding of what it means to organize, delegate and follow-up. I wish every Sacred Heart girl could have the experience."[44] Mary Leddy and Sheila Donahue from Bloomfield Hills and Karen Hagnell of Sheridan Road all felt that the confidence they gained from the practical training at the workshop had helped them function as effective and responsible leaders. Candi Bond of Villa Duchesne wrote: "The various skills which I learned have been an extremely valuable aid in organizing and planning activities for the good of the student body, as well as for the faculty and administration. This accomplishment is a reflection of what the Society of the Sacred Heart calls 'leadership for service and for the common good.'"

Our provincial archives in St. Louis, Missouri, contain a list of meetings held each year in which gatherings and projects were discussed. But listing them all here is not my purpose. Rather, I hope to capture the sense of creativity, new life and birth that was engendered during these early years of the Network of Sacred Heart Schools. This was particularly important and life-giving, the Network coming as it did after the recent period of school closings and upheaval in the United States. We must remember that these were challenging and painful days for many RSCJ. As they said goodbye to sisters who were choosing to leave religious life, they were simultaneously trying to explain to their lay constituencies the changes in the Church and religious life resulting from Vatican II. Our lives combined an unusual and at times irreconcilable mixture of excitement over new, evolving ministries and profound grieving, as we said goodbye to colleagues and much loved schools.

"EDUCATION AS SACRAMENT"

A major source of such new life was the affirmation we all received from working with David Purpel of the University of North Carolina at Greensboro. David was an educator, a scholar, and the author of the still relevant book *The Moral and Spiritual Crisis in Education*. In 1991, he

---

[44] All quotes taken from *Network News*, Volume 1, Number 1, May 1983.

contributed an article to *Independent School* magazine entitled "Education as Sacrament," in which he contrasted education within the Sacred Heart network with education as represented by people concerned primarily with the competitive place of American schools in a world viewed as a market place. Dr. Purpel's primary vision was that education is about making or not making a better world.

> What is truly remarkable and inspiring about the efforts of the Society of the Sacred Heart and its Network is that they represent one of the very few approaches, and maybe the only one, that constitutes a serious alternative to existing educational models. I have not seen any statement that integrates an education policy with a spiritual vision as well as the present Sacred Heart documents do. Nor have I seen any group as serious as the Society in its determination to carry out ideas of such profound significance. Significant efforts to transform education as reflected in the reports of the Society of the Sacred Heart provide us with the exhilarating opportunity to define ourselves, not as pedagogues, bureaucrats and experts, but as participants in the sacred covenant to create a world of justice, love, and meaning.

His endorsement provided very helpful energy and motivated us to go further in our efforts to provide truly excellent education.

REGIONAL MEETINGS

For teachers new to Sacred Heart education the Network held regional meetings each fall. Ideally, during the first three years of working in a Sacred Heart school, new employees were required to attend one of those meetings. Not only did these gatherings introduce all employees to working under the auspices of the Goals and Criteria and the history and heritage of Sacred Heart education, they were also designed to cultivate relationships between and among schools and to promote a sense of working within a Network that stretched, in fact, across the globe. The regions coincided with the five Provinces that existed at that time across the United States: the California Province, the Chicago Province, the Southern Province, the New York Province and the Washington Province. The archives provided me with a good sample of the agenda of such a meeting. One, held in Menlo Park in the California Province (comprising schools in Seattle, San Francisco, and Menlo Park, now Atherton), began on a Friday afternoon with a presentation by Sister Cora McLaughlin on the history of Sacred Heart education. This was followed by a panel of experienced Sacred Heart educators: Mr. Leo Hogan from our San Francisco school, Mrs. Mary Moeschler from Forest Ridge in Bellevue, Washington, near Seattle, and Mrs. Barbara Berkowitz from Menlo Park. The following morning Sister Ann Conroy, then Head of School in San Francisco, gave a presentation on Education as Mission; Sister Sandy Theunick, Head of School at Forest Ridge, spoke on the religious dimensions of Sacred Heart education; and Sister Clare McGowan, from Stone Ridge in Bethesda, Maryland, spoke on our tradition of academic excellence. An alumnae panel then discussed the effects of Sacred Heart education on their lives. The following morning, I spoke about the Goals and Criteria, and the meeting closed with time for school groups to get together and plan how to share their experience with their own school communities upon their return.

THE NOTRE DAME PROGRAM

As mentioned in Part I, the five Provincials and Directors of Education in each of the five Provinces realized that it was important to identify possible future leaders for our schools in the United States and to give them training. In this way, they would be prepared to lead not only excellent independent schools, but schools that promoted the values articulated in the Goals and Criteria. Sister Collins developed a key relationship with leaders of the Masters Program in Educational Administration at the University of Notre Dame, and there ensued a wonderful partnership. Participants in this program combined rigorous coursework at Notre Dame during several summers with something Sister Collins called "Society Seminars." These were led by both Religious of the Sacred Heart and other religious and educational leaders, and were designed to deepen participants' understanding of the vision of Sacred Heart education and the evolution of that vision at that moment in history.

Thirty-two educators were invited by the five Provincials to attend this program and receive an MEA from the University of Notre Dame. For the most part, the participants were Sacred Heart sisters, but—pointing clearly to the future—several lay teachers and administrators also received invitations. This program began at LaSalle College in Philadelphia in the summer of 1975 and then moved to Notre Dame for its final three years. Examples of the many excellent Society Seminar topics and leaders included the following: *Justice and the Church* by Mr. Joe Holland from the Center of Concern in Washington, D.C.; *The Society of the Sacred Heart through its General Chapters of 1964-1976* by Sisters Jean Ford, Catherine Lacey, Kit Collins and Mavie Coakley; *The World and the Adolescent* by Dr. Marvin Schwartz; *How and Why Groups Change* by Sister Jean Bartunek; *Education and the Role of Women* by Sister Mary Quinlan; *The Development and Use of Resources for Mission* by Sister Nance O'Neil; and *The Search for Integrity Essential to Sacred Heart Education* by Reverend Roger Radloff.

THE EXCHANGE PROGRAM

At the same time, Sister Collins, with the energetic assistance of Sister Magee Cappelli, members of the School Committee, and the Network Office staff, put a great deal of thought and energy into the development of a national and international student exchange program. Before the term *Global Citizen* became a catch phrase, Sacred Heart schools proved to be natural laboratories for promoting a sense of belonging to a world beyond one's own borders. Initially high school students, usually during their sophomore year, left their home school for a significant segment of a school year. They would stay in the home of a student in the host school, and in most cases a return visit on the part of that host student would occur. Exchange Coordinators in each school facilitated the program, arranging visits and coordinating students' academic classes from one school to another.

A move was also under way to research international exchanges, which would begin before the end of the decade. This program now takes place in many different ways for both individual students and school groups that travel to other parts of the world for a variety of reasons.

NATIONAL TRUSTEES CONFERENCES

In 1982, as planned by the members of the Interprovincial Board, the Society of the Sacred Heart in the United States did, in fact, become one Province, bringing together religious from coast to coast and north to south. This only strengthened the sense of national unity among the community of Sacred Heart Network educators. At the same time, another important constituency was added to the Network programs.

In October of 1982, the Network held its first National Trustees Conference at the 4-H Center in Washington, D.C. This is a gathering that has continued annually to this day. Its purpose is to introduce trustees and Heads of School to our Sacred Heart heritage, and to help them lead their schools not just as successful businesses, but according to the Goals and Criteria. Case studies were the most common and successful tool used at these early trustee conferences in order to illustrate the unique nature of Sacred Heart education. Many trustees had served previously on other boards, so the focus of these conferences was to imbue them with an understanding of the Goals and Criteria and the importance of leading their schools while embracing this profound sense of leadership as *mission*.[45] As time went on and relationships deepened, trustees began to call one another, meet with one another when traveling to one another's cities, and in general adopt a belief that the Network belonged to them, together with the RSCJ. It soon became obvious that boards of trustees would play an increasingly important role in the development of the Network of Sacred Heart Schools.

Between the national conferences, Sister Collins worked with a small group of trustees called the Core Trustees. This committee consisted of three trustees and three Heads of School from various Sacred Heart schools. The committee planned the annual trustees' conferences and researched possible national projects such as a national medical insurance plan and national fundraising for the schools. I was a member of that

---

[45] One is reminded here of the earliest days of Sacred Heart education, when Madeleine Sophie was training religious who had previously been part of monastic orders and often took some time to adapt to her new vision of a "wholly apostolic, wholly contemplative" Society.

group, which proved to be particularly helpful when I became the Network Coordinator in 1984.

As we look back on these years of such sadness in closing so many schools and yet such joy in the birth and creativity of the Network of Sacred Heart Schools, it is clear that the spirited and inspiring leadership of Sister Collins left behind an extraordinary legacy. In remembering those days, I think of Sister Collins' intelligence and wit, her wonderful sense of humor, and most of all her insistence on including all in the creation of the Goals and Criteria. Her singular ability to move the schools through a period of unmatched upheaval and loss cannot be underestimated.

I close this chapter with a quotation from the *Harvard Business Review* that was one of her favorites:

> A network was a number of individuals who, while they had no formal operational relationship with each other, had nevertheless such a close understanding and powerful informal relationship that the connection was a force to be reckoned with in the affairs of the country.

Kit Collins herself was indeed a force to be reckoned with. There is little doubt that without the kind of leadership she provided at this pivotal moment, the Network of Sacred Heart Schools may not have survived— much less become the powerful force it is today. Out of a fledgling organization of schools, she enabled the emergence of a synergistic whole that far exceeds the sum of its parts.

Sister Collins died suddenly on March 14, 2010. Her legacy continues to inspire us.

CHAPTER 7

The Network Directed
by Sister Susan Maxwell
1984–1995

I was standing in the dessert line at the second annual Trustees Conference in Washington, D.C., in October of 1983, when Sister Nance O'Neil came up behind me and said she wanted me to be the next Coordinator of the Network. We then talked of other things. Little did I imagine that she meant I would leave Bloomfield Hills and start this new position the following summer! But in January of 1984, Sister O'Neil arrived in Detroit and told the school community of my new position, scheduled to start the following summer. Thus began eleven challenging and rewarding years.

(l. to r.) Sisters Maxwell and Collins, 1998

THE SCHOOL COMMITTEE

I inherited from Sister Collins many important components of the position. Most significant among them was the School Committee, which consisted of three Heads of School and three middle managers (usually division heads of the upper, middle or lower schools). This committee's agenda proceeded from an excellent proposal form that could be submitted by anyone working in a Network school who wished to suggest a topic for a national meeting: curriculum directors, business managers, division heads, and so on. The committee met several times a year to process such proposals and to determine who on the School Committee would become the "tracker" and help to make such meetings or projects a success.

An example of such a gathering appears in the School Committee Report of June 1985. There it is reported that Jackie Martin, the curriculum director of our Sacred Heart School in Grand Coteau, Louisiana, proposed a meeting of the upper school curriculum directors during the national meeting of the Association for Supervision and Curriculum Development (ASCD) in San Francisco the following year. Jackie Martin would contact the curriculum directors with details and coordinate their efforts while Sister Anne Dyer became the School Committee tracker. Such proposals came frequently, and the support and assistance of a School Committee member as a tracker assured the success of each meeting or project. From the elementary heads meeting at the Kino Learning Center in Tucson, Arizona, to the traveling art show of student work that made its way around the Network Schools in the late spring of 1985 to the publication of Sister Jan Dunn's new edition of "Life at the Sacred Heart," the School Committee was never to meet without having a full agenda of proposals.

THE ST. PHILIPPINE DUCHESNE BANNERS PROJECT

In January of 1988, the School Committee gathered for its annual Miami meeting.[46] During the meeting, I received a phone call from Sister O'Neil. In her typically engaging way, she said she would love the School Committee to find a way to have a banner from each of our schools at the

---

[46] The Committee always met in different Network locations in order to get to know the different schools and their communities; Miami, however, was a must for the January meeting each year!

canonization of Rose Philippine Duchesne that was to take place in Rome that July. After some discussion—and in her usual positive way—Mrs. Mary Moeschler volunteered to be the tracker for this project. Recently I asked her to share her memories of the Banners Project and she sent this excellent account.

> I volunteered to track this endeavor knowing that Mike Saito, Chair of Forest Ridge's art department and a dear friend, would courageously and confidently take leadership of this incredible production. Mike wrote a letter to each of the nineteen Sacred Heart schools asking that a sketch for its banner be submitted by March 1. The flags would reflect the school's unique identity and mirror how Philippine impacted the vitality of their local community. He described the measurements of the banner, the colors and fabric that would be used to create a rainbow effect when they were all raised on high, but left the creative details of each piece of art up to each individual school.

Mary went on to explain how Mike contacted Mr. Michael Red Earth, a graphic designer from High Flying Banners in Seattle, who would actually create the flags. She commented that Philippine works in many remarkable ways—and that in this case she had outdone herself. "When Mr. S and I arrived at High Flying Banners for our first meeting with Michael Red Earth, I explained that one of the founding mothers of the Society of the Sacred Heart would be canonized in Rome on July 3, 1988, by Pope John Paul II. Mr. Red Earth asked me to tell him something about this French-born nun. When he learned that she had longed to work with Native Americans, his eyes glistened, and he said, 'I want to read everything I can about this pioneer woman!' And so he did!"

A Pacific Northwest Native American, Mr. Red Earth embraced the spirit of Philippine, who always dreamed big, and his completed banners beautifully represented the nineteen schools.

Meanwhile, Sister O'Neil had arranged for each school to send two representatives to Rome for the canonization. Mike Saito and his wife, Karen, also traveled to Italy with banners, poles, and pole pockets and then oversaw the procession of the colorful flags being carried into St. Peter's Square. Vatican security would not allow them to enter the basilica for fear that weapons could be hidden in their folds, but they certainly led the way on that day. Mike always spoke of this project as a journey in many ways. As very young children, both he and his wife had spent time in a Japanese-American internment camp on the West Coast. When he and Karen came home to Seattle after the canonization, they entered into an RCIA program at St. James Cathedral. On Holy Saturday, 1990, Mike and Karen became Catholics. Again, in Mary's eloquent words, Philippine's spirit inspired two of her children to "step gently over despair and fashion a resurrection realm, a hope-hallowed world."

CONRAD HILTON GRANTS

The School Committee reports following each meeting are filled with information regarding various projects and meetings taking place within the Network in those years. One project came to fruition after I received a phone call from Sister O'Neil saying that she had heard from Steve Hilton, the grandson of Conrad Hilton. Steve stated that his grandfather had given him very clear instructions to follow after his grandfather's death. He was to reach out to the Sisters of Loretto, who had raised Conrad in one of their orphanages, and to the Religious of the Sacred Heart because of the excellent relationships he had developed with the RSCJ at Barat College in Lake Forest, Illinois. Steve was to find out what the sisters needed at the time of Conrad's death. Sister O'Neil and I had spoken frequently about how to promote social justice and find a way for our schools to live St. Madeleine Sophie's commitment to the poor—something that, as mentioned previously, she herself had lived through establishing a free school or its equivalent on the property of every one of her academies. Sister O'Neil instructed Steve Hilton to call me and find a way to move forward with this commitment. Steve and I had several conversations and decided that part of his grandfather's estate would include a $50,000 donation to be distributed by the School Committee to individual Network schools that would submit proposals outlining how they would develop a service program in their school. This generous grant was renewed in the two subsequent years, and the schools developed very thoughtful and creative service programs with the Hilton funding of $150,000. This portion of Conrad Hilton's estate has since become the Conrad Hilton Sisters' Fund, which provides funding for many excellent programs for a wide variety of religious congregations around the world.

THE NETWORK SUMMER PROJECTS

During the 1980s, Sister Sheila Hammond, then the Director of Novices, and some of her novices met with me to discuss a Network program that has stood the test of time: the Network Summer Projects. The vision for this program, in the spirit of the original Network vision to provide programs for every constituency in the schools, was to provide opportunities in the summer months for Network high school students to gather in one particular school, to live there very simply, to pray together and to provide service in some meaningful way in their host city or suburb. That first summer we provided a program in one location; by the summer of 2016 summer programs took place in fifteen different locations. Over these many years, such programs have provided rich educational opportunities, not only for students, but also for the faculty and staff members who have accompanied them.

FIRST REVISION OF THE GOALS AND CRITERIA—AND A PARADIGM SHIFT

In the late 1980s from around the Network came the clear perception that it was time to review and update the Goals and Criteria of 1975. This was true for two reasons: the need to change the wording of Criteria that used exclusive language, and the call to include among the Criteria new insights about environmental and health education.[47]

---

[47] Goal 1 was the only actual *Goal* whose wording changed: the 1975 version had stated, "Schools of the Sacred Heart commit themselves to educate to a faith that is relevant in a secularized world" while the 1990 version stated that "Schools of the Sacred Heart commit themselves to educate to a personal and active faith in God." New Criteria included: under Goal One, "The school teaches respect for the various religious traditions of the world"; under Goal Two, "The curriculum prepares students to live cooperatively in a global and technological society"; under Goal Three, "The curriculum includes the study of the welfare of the Earth and its limited resources," "The school is linked in a reciprocal manner with ministries with the poor and marginalized," and "The allocation of the school's resources reflects

But for those of us on the School Committee, the most striking experience during this process was the clear shift—a real paradigm shift!—from teaching three-to eighteen-year-olds about the values articulated within the Goals and Criteria to enlisting the *adults* in each Sacred Heart community to live and model these values. This shift in emphasis is quite possibly the key to the Goals' having thrived so completely in the more than twenty-five years since this revision. Perhaps no greater addition took place during the course of this period in the history of the Network. Rather than a mission statement tucked carefully in a drawer, every year the adult communities in every Sacred Heart school are called to articulate the next best steps for them to *live* and *model* the values expressed in the Goals and Criteria.

At each School Committee meeting between 1988 and 1990, we reviewed draft after draft of suggestions that came to us from every school community as well as from every religious community of RSCJ. By the time our work was completed in 1990, Sister Rosemary Bearss had become the Provincial of our United States Province. She and I decided it was important to introduce this new articulation of the Goals and Criteria using our national teleconference system so that each school had a way to include its entire school community in this exciting national event. Students, faculty, staff and in some cases parents and alums gathered in gymnasiums across the county. A slide show of every school accompanied the formal reading of the revised Goals and Criteria. Each school also contributed a prayerful intention. I remember well the call I received from the teleconference operator just after we completed the teleconference. He exclaimed with great excitement, "Do you realize we just had more than ten thousand people listening to that call?" I still have alumnae/i approach me with memories of that national technological gathering.

Some years later in 1995, several of us participated at the annual meeting of the National Catholic Education Association in Cincinnati. There, after he had finished delivering his paper, a very good Jesuit friend,

---

the values of the Goals and Criteria"; under Goal Four, "The adults model and teach skills needed to build community, and provide opportunities to exercise those skills" and "Laity and religious join as colleagues in the mission of Sacred Heart education"; under Goal Five, "The school educates to a lifelong sense of responsibility for health and well-being."

Howard Gray, SJ, drew me aside and reemphasized the importance of adult modeling—witnessing rather than preaching to young people. He said to me, "The vision that you people have that is so important has to do with modeling." We know that teaching values to young people is not sufficient. We must live, give strong evidence of, the values we hope to pass on to the next generation.

INTRODUCTION OF SCHOOL HEADS AND BOARD CHAIRS AS NETWORK DECISION MAKERS

Before she completed her terms as the first Provincial of the United States Province, Sister O'Neil and I spoke frequently about the fact that my position should no longer be one of simply staff to the Provincial. Rather, we agreed that the Network Coordinator should also be responsible to Boards of Trustees and Heads of School. Recent experience had shown that the future of Sacred Heart education was not only in the hands of the Provincial and her Team, but also in the hands of Board Chairs and their board members, and Heads of School and their administrative teams, faculties and staffs. This new vision was first articulated in a paper entitled "Network Planning" in 1986, which is available at our archives in St. Louis.

In the spring of 1987 the Provincial Team, Board Chairs, and Heads of School gathered for the first time. At the second meeting in 1988, a significant vote took place in which all three parties agreed to bring to birth a structure that would be charged with planning for the Network of the future. Sister Rosemary Bearss and I selected three Heads of School and three Board Chairs to develop the details for this new educational entity. It was clear to all of us that responsibility for living the Society's mission in each school would rest with the Provincial and her team through the Commission on Goals. A Network Board consisting of the Provincial, Heads or former Heads of School, and Trustees or former Trustees would be responsible to hire the Network Director Coordinator and oversee Network programs. Of paramount importance was the decision that such programs would be directly related to the mission of Sacred Heart education and never duplicate offerings from other national educational organizations. Meanwhile, gatherings for new Network trustees had continued every October since 1982.

The Network structure—New Trustees Meetings in the fall, and decision-making meetings in the spring—has since been revised several times, consistently honoring the importance of the Goals and Criteria as the expression of the Society's charism. In addition, each revision has safeguarded the appropriate role of the Provincial in monitoring the life of that vision in each school; the role of the Boards of Trustees in assuring strong resources for living that vision; and the role of Heads of School in making that vision live in a strong and real way on each campus.

When I think of those years, I realize that a driving influence for all of us was the critical insight that the Network does indeed belong to all involved. It was important that Religious of the Sacred Heart be free to work in Network schools or in another apostolate, according to their call. This was made possible by the increasing awareness that the charism of the Society, as expressed in the Goals and Criteria, could be carried forward effectively by and with our lay colleagues.

It was at this time that Donat Marchand, a trustee of the Sacred Heart school in Greenwich, Connecticut, articulated the importance of each group of adults in a Sacred Heart school. In the same article referenced in Chapter 1,[48] he makes a clear case for educating trustees to the values of the Society's charism and honoring their role in this three-fold responsibility for the future of Sacred Heart education:

> While the day-to-day affairs are in the hands primarily of their faculty members and to a lesser extent of their administration, it is of course the trustees who bear the responsibility for the long-term future. It is the trustees who make the final decisions in selecting a president, i.e. Head of School, and at whose pleasure the president then serves; it is the trustees who safeguard and, in the best cases, increase the endowment; it is the trustees who support the president, where the buck usually stops, and who can buffer the institution against outside interference, whether from the local community, inflamed alumni, or state and national government. *The trustees are the ultimate goalies.*

---

[48] RSCJ Newsletter, July 1988.

To this end, Sister Anne Dyer contributed an excellent tool for reviewing the effectiveness of both School Heads and Boards of Trustees. This booklet is entitled *Evaluating the Head and Board of Trustees in a Sacred Heart School* and is worth reviewing for use in Sacred Heart Schools today.[49]

THE NATIONAL FACULTY DEVELOPMENT COMMITTEE

Meanwhile another voice was raised in the chorus of those who were key to the present life and educational success in the future of Sacred Heart education in the United States: the experienced faculty members. Upon becoming Coordinator of the Network, I inherited a committee of experienced teachers that had been selected by Sister Collins but had not yet met with her to discuss and determine their place and role within the Network. At our first meeting, the teachers and I reached an important decision. Rather than assuming that we alone could determine the role of such a new committee, we realized that these veteran teachers needed to meet personally with experienced teachers in every Sacred Heart school in order to discover and articulate what it was that had made them embrace Sacred Heart education. From there, we worked to develop meaningful programs that would help others to do so.

I can still remember our surprise as we heard the consistent answers that came from all around the United States. First, experienced faculty valued Sacred Heart education because there was far less red tape than they had experienced working in other schools. They also agreed that key to their embracing of our educational charism was their ability to develop a meaningful relationship with a long-term Sacred Heart educator, whether lay or religious. Finally, and of greatest interest to me and our committee, they all felt that they had found a philosophical or spiritual home in the Goals and Criteria. In fact, they said, our Goals and Criteria expressed in words what they had understood to be their way to find meaning in life, regardless of their religious denomination or cultural background. Thus, in a way we never could have anticipated, the role of the experienced faculty became one of ever deepening reflection on and articulation of the charism

---

[49] Available in the provincial archives in St. Louis.

of the Society of the Sacred Heart. This took place in two major ways: the *Network Journal of Education*, which included a wide variety of articles by Sacred Heart teachers; and Faculty Institutes, gatherings of teachers from across the country around a variety of topics. Soon this committee evolved into the NFDC, the Network Faculty Development Committee, under the leadership of Sister Catherine Lacey and Diane Wood, experienced educators who had each served in a variety of Sacred Heart schools.

The *Network Journal of Education*—unlike the *Network News*, a publication that emerged directly from the Network office and included newsworthy articles from every Sacred Heart School—was a serious pedagogical journal that invited faculty and staff to consider both theory and practice as they wrote about a particular program or project. The editorial board was headed by Sister Catherine Lacey, who had recently served on the staff of the *Harvard Educational Review*. Working with her, a board of five educators, each representing a different Network school, culled submissions from Sacred Heart faculty and staff across the country. The journal was published between 1990 and 1997 and featured articles that connected current pedagogical issues and challenges with the Goals and Criteria. One can easily imagine how such a journal might function on-line today.

At the same time, the NFDC developed a plan for sponsoring Faculty Institutes. In July of 1993, they held a national institute with 70 participants from all 19 schools. In the summer of 1994, they held both a southern and a western regional meeting; in the summer of 1995, an eastern and a midwestern institute followed. We have an excellent evaluation of these institutes, which can be found in the provincial archives.

I asked Sister Shirley Miller to share some of her memories of those days. At the time of the NFDC, she was the Head of School at the Rosary in New Orleans. "I have lots of memories of the faculty development work and all that we did at the Rosary, naming ourselves ESCJ[50] and having t-shirts made for all of the faculty and staff. That was probably 1990, and it continued strong into 2003 when I left." Sister Miller went on to explain how faculty and staff were encouraged to sign up for various committees, one of them involving formation to mission and Society history (including

---

[50] An acronym for "Educateurs du Sacré Cœur de Jésus" (tr: Educators of the Sacred Heart of Jesus), explicitly identifying lay educators with the RSCJ (Religieuses du Sacré Cœur de Jésus).

things like trips to Sugar Creek, St. Charles and St. Marys, Kansas). "The whole point was to distribute leadership among all the adults," she said, "to get buy-in, to build a strong community of faith, and to encourage adults to take responsibility for the climate of the school." The success of the Faculty Development Committees in the schools depended, of course, on the extent to which Heads of School were comfortable entrusting employees with this level of responsibility. Sister Jean Bartunek, a professor of Organizational Development at Boston College whose interests center around academic-practitioner relationships and organizational change, was taken enough with the success of the National Committee's work that she featured the NFDC in her book *Organizational and Educational Change: The Life and Role of a Change Agent Group*.[51]

CONCLUSION

When I think of those eleven years, so filled with challenges, life and energy, I recall words of Henri Nouwen that I frequently cited in my talks with Network communities. Its message is certainly needed in today's world:

> To build a better world, the beginnings of that world must be visible in daily life – here and now. There is no reason to expect much to happen in the future if the signs of hope are not visible in the present. We cannot speak about ways to bring about peace and freedom if we cannot draw from our own experience of peace and freedom here and now. We cannot commit ourselves to work for justice and love in tomorrow's society if we cannot discover the seeds of these in the relationships we engage ourselves in today. When schools are places where community can be experienced, where people can live together without fear of each other, and learning can be based on a creative exchange of experiences and ideas, then there is a chance that those who come from them will have an increasing desire to bring about in the world what they have experienced in their years of formation. In this sense, schools are not training camps to prepare people to enter into a violent society, but places where redemptive forms of society

---

[51] 2003, Mahwah, N.J.: Lawrence Erlbaum Associates.

can be experimented with and offered to the modern world as alternative styles of life.

As Sacred Heart education moves forward into the twenty-first century, it seems most important that each school continue to take seriously this call to discern how best to live the mission of the Society as expressed today in the Goals and Criteria. As in the day of St. Madeleine Sophie, we do so in the light of our changing world as well as the particular circumstances of each school. Experience has taught us that we can embrace that challenge best and most profoundly as a community of committed educators.

AFTERWORD

From the present vantage point of 2017, two realities of the first twenty-five years of the Network of Sacred Heart Schools stand out for me.

First, the Goals and Criteria, now in their third iteration of 2005. Unlike most mission statements for schools and organizations, the Goals and Criteria move from a theoretical philosophical statement to concrete objectives. One can never check off that he or she has "finished with" a particular Goal or Criterion. There is always a next best step for oneself or for a particular institution. Thus, an ongoing lived reality describes the environment of any Sacred Heart School. The evolution of a school community and its priorities takes place within the evolution of our world and its achievements, tragedies, and challenges.

Secondly, Sister Kit Collins' visionary leadership, which enabled a broad and real sense of ownership of the Goals and Criteria. From 1973 to 1975, she worked with an ever changing group of Heads of Sacred Heart Schools, both lay and religious, to write draft after draft of that document. She insisted that every religious community and every school community contribute to those drafts. To this day, I still have Sacred Heart educators stop me to explain that their school community was responsible for a particular criterion. This highly inclusive process has been true as well for subsequent editions of the Goals and Criteria. The Sacred Heart Commission on Goals and Network programs and projects have enabled this sense of ownership to grow from the nineteen schools that made up the Network in 1995 to the twenty-four institutions that today embrace this articulation of a healthy, profound philosophy of life.

With so much gratitude, I am confident that Sacred Heart education will continue to be a key player in that large, diverse community of people around the world who are committed in so many ways to offering young people the very best possible education.

I conclude by quoting from an article I wrote almost twenty years ago—but which seems to have accrued even more relevance for the world in which we find ourselves today.

> Recently I find myself reflecting more often and more deeply upon the reality that so many of the world's wars and trouble spots are intimately connected to religious beliefs. Closely connected with strong denominational attachments, of course, are those that are ethnic in nature and origin. It seems obvious that if the human race is to survive, grow, evolve to its next stage, a profound shift is needed. Human beings will need to respond as the young diarist, Zlata, from Sarajevo did when asked by her American talk show host about her citizenship. Zlata answered that she is a citizen of the earth.
>
> We have so much experience in our Network schools of people young and old finding their spiritual homes with us, no matter what their denominational affiliations might be. As our culture experiences the emptiness of a purely secular, materialistic existence, and our world is ravaged by the destruction of fanatical denominationalism, we cannot afford to take lightly the contribution we have to offer.
>
> I believe that there is a very real connection between our particular approach to religion and the foundation that is needed for a world community. Let us help one another to make those connections on the local, regional, and national levels. Then let us tell our stories of a lived faith that, in fact, does cut across all barriers. There is a strength in that faith that I believe we have only begun to articulate for each other and for our time.

APPENDIX

To date, there have been three editions of the Goals and Criteria, in 1975, 1990 and 2005. The reader can see that each edition shows growth in understanding how an individual or an institution can give evidence of living each of the Goals of Sacred Heart education, a healthy philosophy pf life.

Goals and Criteria
1975

Schools of the Sacred Heart commit themselves to educate to:

- faith which is relevant in a secularized world
- a deep respect for intellectual values
- a social awareness which impels to action
- the building of community as a Christian value
- personal growth in an atmosphere of wise freedom

PREAMBLE

to the Goals and Criteria for Sacred Heart Schools in the United States

The schools of the Sacred Heart in the United States, members of a worldwide network, offer an education that is marked by a distinctive spirit. It is of the essence of a Sacred Heart school that it be deeply concerned for each student's total development: spiritual, intellectual, emotional, physical. It is of the essence of a Sacred Heart school that it emphasize serious study, that it educate to social responsibility, and that it lay the foundations of a strong faith.

Many educators, especially Christian educators, will find much that they can identify with in the stated purposes of Sacred Heart schools. Given the vast needs of the world, of the Church in the United States, of children and their parents, it should be cause for rejoicing that this is so, that many seek to meet these complex challenges in a similar fashion. But what will always be distinctive about the schools of the Sacred Heart is the long tradition from which they come. This tradition, which has permeated the training of the Religious of the Sacred Heart, is familiar to the Religious who teach in the schools, but perhaps less familiar to the lay colleagues who work so closely with them. It has been experientially familiar to generations of Sacred Heart students who, as alumnae, send their children to receive the education they themselves valued so highly.

For the Religious of the Sacred Heart, education has always been viewed as a *mission* of the most demanding kind.[52] "The Religious of the Sacred Heart are consecrated by their vocation to education." Members of the Society drew up the first *Plan of Studies* in 1805, five years after their own founding, and reformulated it ten times over the next 150 years. Sacred Heart Schools first held to a single, uniform curriculum, but in 1958 a document significantly entitled *Spirit and Plan of Studies* "deliberately puts aside all details of syllabus" noting that "these are bound to vary according to time and place," and tries to "give a clear idea of a spirit...which will hold good for every work of education"[53] that the Society might undertake.

If one seeks the timeless element in Sacred Heart education, one must look to that spirit, for externals and customs were always seen as subject to change. Timelessness has never meant rigid adherence to a single program or method. Revision of curriculum was always a concern of the Society's General Congregations, which had the highest decision-making authority in the Order.

> Whatever the orientation given to studies may be, there must
> be no forgetting that it means the formation of the whole

---

[52] Constitutions of the Society of the Sacred Heart, 1815, III, 4, i.
[53] Spirit and Plan of Studies, p. 7.

woman with a view to her own vocation in the circumstances and the age in which she has to live.[54]

The present paper resembles others in which, since 1967, the Society of the Sacred Heart has defined itself and its mission in the contemporary Church. Like these, it does not pretend to say the last word on its subject. Like these, it draws upon the texts of the Second Vatican Council, for it is in the Sacred Heart tradition to be deeply loyal to the Church and to respond swiftly to the challenges and opportunities the Church offers. For this reason, the evolution of schools of the Sacred Heart makes little sense if viewed outside the context of the history of the Catholic Church.

In the last ten years the American schools of the Sacred Heart, following the spirit of the Society and of the Church, have adapted their programs and methods to suit the special situation of each school. The decentralization of control, which made this possible, was embarked upon in full confidence that the presence of Religious of the Sacred Heart alone would (so it was assumed) assure that the essentials of Sacred Heart education would be preserved.

It is never safe, however, to assume too much. Values taken for granted or left unarticulated can become inoperative. Patterns of leadership and governance, the make-up of faculties and student bodies have changed rapidly, and as the schools of the Sacred Heart enter the mainstream of American independent education, they feel its characteristic pressures and strains. As they become increasingly diverse, it becomes increasingly necessary to respond to the question: "What makes a Sacred Heart school?" Independent but never isolated, every Sacred Heart school needs to feel the strength of belonging to a larger whole, of sharing principles and values, broad purposes, hopes and ambitions.

The following pages attempt to delineate what a Sacred Heart school is in the 1970's. They draw upon the Society's basic documents, as well as working papers recently developed by the Heads of Schools. This paper therefore repeats much that will be familiar to Religious of the Sacred Heart and to those close to the Society in recent years.

Five *Goals* are stated, and several *Criteria* are given for each. The first three Goals are taken directly from the section on education in the

---

[54] Plan, p. 13.

documents of the Society's 1970 General Chapter. The Criteria are signs which indicate that the Goal is being effectively pursued.

The Goals and Criteria are *sine qua non* for every school that belongs to the Sacred Heart network. They provide the framework within which each school is to develop specific *Objectives* appropriate to its local situation. Means of evaluation and accountability have also been designed, so that each school, and the network as a whole, may draw maximum benefit from this process.

Approved by the Interprovincial Board
April 26, 1975

GOAL I

FAITH WHICH IS RELEVANT IN A SECULARIZED WORLD

Criteria for Goal I:
1. The school recognizes its life force in the love of Jesus Christ by supporting in concrete ways the value of reflection and of prayer.
2. The total educational program affirms the belief that there is meaning in life and thereby fosters within the school community a sense of hope.
3. The religious studies program probes the relationship of God to man and to the world.
4. The school provides education to decision making in the light of Christian principles.
5. The school presents itself to the wider community as a Christ-centered institution within the evolving tradition of the Church.

GOAL II

A DEEP RESPECT FOR INTELLECTUAL VALUES

Criteria for Goal II:
1. The course of study is intellectually challenging.
2. Serious study and a love of learning are encouraged.
3. Program development is based on research and evaluation.
4. Teaching/learning styles promote the development of persons who are knowledgeable, questioning, thoughtful and integrated.
5. Opportunities are provided for experiential education, which includes the element of reflection.
6. The curriculum encourages the development of aesthetic values and the creative use of the imagination.

GOAL III

A SOCIAL AWARENESS WHICH IMPELS TO ACTION

Criteria for Goal III:
1. The school awakens a critical sense, which leads to reflection on our society and its values.
2. The curriculum includes study of the problems of the world community.
3. The school provides the knowledge and skills needed for effective action on the problems of oppression and injustice.
4. The school has programs which enable students to become actively involved in the wider community.

GOAL IV

THE BUILDING OF COMMUNITY AS A CHRISTIAN VALUE

Criteria for Goal IV:
1. Skills needed to build community are taught and opportunities to exercise those skills are provided.
2. School policies and practices are established and reviewed in the light of Christian principles.
3. The school provides experiences of diversity, which are designed to develop an understanding and appreciation of various races, religions and cultures.
4. An effective financial aid program supports socio-economic diversity.
5. The life of the school community is deepened by an understanding of the purposes and evolving tradition of Sacred Heart education.
6. The school participates actively in the national and international network of Sacred Heart schools.
7. The program is designed to help students take their place as responsible citizens in an interdependent world.

GOAL V

PERSONAL GROWTH IN AN ATMOSPHERE OF WISE FREEDOM

Criteria for Goal V

1. Genuine concern for each member of the school community is a priority.
2. Students learn to deal with their gifts and limitations in a growth-producing way.
3. Students are helped to share their knowledge and gifts with others.
4. School policies and practices further the development of self-discipline.
5. The school provides for the development of leadership.

GOALS AND CRITERIA OF 1990

INTRODUCTION

The 1975 Goals and Criteria articulated the essence of a Sacred Heart school in the United States. For the past fifteen years the commitment to educate to these five goals has defined a Sacred Heart school and has bound it to the other schools in the Network in a common mission. Today, on the edge of the third millennium, many Network colleagues have experienced the need to again refocus and rearticulate our educational priorities.

As we approach the twenty-first century, Sacred Heart schools in the United States "have a new appreciation of their potential to participate in a radical reshaping of society."[55] This 1990 expression recognizes the perennial institutional issues: tradition and change, continuity and reform, society and the individual. The challenge, however, continues to lie in the five elements that have been the framework of Sacred Heart education since its beginning in 1800. These principles are ageless, but the context for the challenge has changed and this requires from us a fresh response.

The needs of the world and of the United States again set the agenda for our response. Family life is in crisis. Economic in equities separate and divide peoples: the gaps continue to increase. Racist attitudes and structures persist. Both men and women struggle to promote the acceptance of the fundamental equality and complementarity of the sexes. Social questions have worldwide dimensions. Violence, drugs, disease, and the destruction of the environment threaten human life and our planet.

The 1990 Goals and Criteria express the values, the intentions, and the hopes of the Sacred Heart tradition, sharpened to meet the needs of a rapidly changing world. They also reflect recent documents of the Society of the Sacred Heart that express the vision of Sacred Heart education and

---

[55] International Education Commission Working Paper, p. 30.

the promise for the future. 'The institutions we hope for today are made up of bonds of relationships between groups of various kinds which have a common value system and policies which allow the promotion of these values. Such institutions interact with the world at large and are able to be called into question from within or without in view of changes in the reality which they are to serve. Members are expected to take real responsibility and to be creative."[56]

The 1990 revision is the result of a year of work on the part of faculty and administration of the nineteen Network schools and the input of many Religious of the Sacred Heart. The revision is rooted in the past and the present and attests to the future. The 1990 Goals challenge us to bring the values of a strong educational tradition to this fragmented world. They will succeed in energizing our mission only in so far as we take bold steps to interpret our local reality and dare to present God's love as a healing and empowering gift.

---

[56] IEC paper, p. 31.

GOAL ONE

Schools of the Sacred Heart commit themselves to educate to a personal and active faith in God.

1. Rooted in the love of Jesus Christ, the school promotes personal and communal prayer, and reflection.
2. The total educational program affirms the belief that there is meaning in life and thereby fosters within the individual and the school community a sense of hope.
3. The school provides education in, and opportunities for, decision making in the light of Gospel values.
4. The religious studies program probes the relationship of self to God, to others, and to the world.
5. The school teaches respect for the various religious traditions of the world.
6. The school presents itself to the wider community as a Christ-centered institution within the evolving tradition of the Church.

GOAL TWO

Schools of the Sacred Heart commit themselves to educate to a deep respect for intellectual values.

1. The course of study offers intellectual challenge and inspires a love of learning.
2. The school develops a curriculum based on the Goals of Sacred Heart education, educational research, and ongoing evaluation.
3. The curriculum prepares students to live cooperatively in a global and technological society.
4. The curriculum develops aesthetic values and the creative use of the imagination.
5. The school provides experiential education which includes elements of reflection, analysis, and synthesis.
6. A variety of approaches to teaching and learning promotes the development of persons who are knowledge able, questioning, thoughtful, and integrated.

7. A program for faculty/staff development, based on the values of Sacred Heart education, furthers the implementation of the Goals.

GOAL THREE

Schools of the Sacred Heart commit themselves to educate to a social awareness which impels to action.

1. The school awakens a critical consciousness that leads its total community to reflect on society and its values.
2. The curriculum includes the study of issues challenging our interdependent world.
3. The curriculum exposes students to the problems of oppression and injustice, and teaches attitudes of peace and behaviors of nonviolence.
4. The curriculum includes the study of the welfare of our earth and its limited resources.
5. The school has programs which enable each member of the school community to be engaged in effective action for social change.
6. The school is linked in a reciprocal manner to ministries with the poor and marginalized.
7. The allocation of the school's resources reflects the values of the *Goals and Criteria.*

GOAL FOUR

Schools of the Sacred Heart commit themselves to educate to the building of community as a Christian value.

1. The adults model and teach skills needed to build community, and provide opportunities to exercise these skills.
2. Laity and religious join as colleagues in the mission of Sacred Heart education.
3. The Board of Trustees and administration establish and review school policies in the light of Christian principles.

4. The financial aid program effectively supports socio economic diversity.
5. The school provides experiences of diversity which develop an understanding and appreciation of all people.
6. An understanding of the purposes, values, and evolving tradition of Sacred Heart education enriches the life of the school community.
7. The school participates actively in the national and inter national network of Sacred Heart schools.
8. The program educates students to assume their role as active and responsible citizens of an interdependent world.

GOAL FIVE

Schools of the Sacred Heart commit themselves to educate to personal growth in an atmosphere of wise freedom.

1. All members of the school community show concern and respect for one another.
2. Students develop self-confidence as they learn to deal realistically with their gifts and limitations.
3. The school structures opportunities for its members to share their knowledge and gifts with others.
4. School policies and practice promote self-discipline, responsibility, and decision malting.
5. School programs provide for the recognition, development, and exercise of leadership in its many forms.
6. The school educates to a life-long sense of responsibility for health and well-being.

The Preamble of the 1975 edition was repeated here.

GOALS AND CRITERIA
FOR SACRED HEART SCHOOLS
IN THE UNITED STATES
2005

INTRODUCTION

The Preamble of the original edition of the *Goals and Criteria* states that "values taken for granted or left unarticulated become inoperative."[57] This conviction resulted in capturing the essence of Sacred Heart education in the five goals and their criteria. The *Goals and Criteria* provide both the uniqueness of a Sacred Heart School and the strong bond of union among the Network of Sacred Heart schools. They continue to challenge all Sacred Heart educators to deepen their understanding of these timeless principles. As the Introduction to the 1990 edition says:

> The challenge, however, continues to live in the five elements that have been the framework of Sacred Heart education since its beginning in 1800. These principles are ageless, but the context for the challenge has changed and this requires of us a fresh response.... The needs of the world and of the United States again set the agenda for our response.[58]

Since that description was written we have crossed the threshold into the third millennium as well as into the third century of Sacred Heart education.

In 2000 the Society of the Sacred Heart held a General Chapter, an international meeting of delegates of its members. Its purpose was to examine the context today for the Society's mission. Through the eyes and experiences of the delegates, the Chapter

---

[57] Preamble to *The Goals and Criteria for Sacred Heart Schools in the United States*, approved by the Interprovincial Board, 1975.

[58] Introduction to *The Goals and Criteria*, approved by the Provincial Team, 1990.

...welcomed into our hearts and into our deliberations the faces of peoples across the globe. We have had before us the faces of hope and promise, the young in their generosity, those who are restless for God, women and men who create and reverence life. We have seen the suffering of children without education, of young people searching for meaning, of those suffering from HIV/AIDS, of women abused and discriminated against, of refugees displaced by war, violence and poverty. These faces of people reveal the Heart of God.[3]

September 11, 2001 forever changed our context. The threat of terrorism in our world, the corporate greed and scandals in our country and a sense of entitlement in its citizens can drain us of hope. At times honesty and integrity in daily life seem to be forgotten virtues. The innovations of technology have connected persons in newer, faster ways, but this instant networking can depersonalize communication. Environmental concerns seem not to get the attention they should be demanding of our governments. Globalization does not always clarify our interdependence; globalization too often brings new burdens for the poor of the world. The Roman Catholic Church finds itself profoundly challenged by internal and external factors. The meaning of faithful membership can sometimes be lost in rhetorical arguments rather than in being firmly rooted in one's relationship with God. The shortage of ordained ministers endangers sacramental life. We recognize we have much to learn about the spiritualities other faith traditions offer.

During the academic year 2004-2005 the constituencies of the Network Schools and the Religious of the Sacred Heart (RSCJ) engaged in a spirited consultation. The *2005 Goals and Criteria Document,* crafted by the Sacred Heart Commission on Goals (SHCOG), is the fruit of this consultation. The "foundational principles" contained in this document are non-negotiable elements for being a Sacred Heart school. It is the expectation that these foundational principles be a part of a school community's reflection when it evaluates its life during the SHCOG process. As with the Criteria, their order in the list does not signify importance; each foundational principle and each criterion is as important as any other one.

The process of refocusing and rearticulating our values as Sacred Heart educators led to many passionate conversations among us. This process of communal reflection has given us renewed appreciation of and commitment to our educational mission and how to live it in today's world. Janet Erskine Stuart, RSCJ, reminds us...

> Epochs of transition must keep us on the alert. They ask us to keep our eyes open upon the distant horizons, our minds listening to seize every indication that can enlighten us; reading, reflexion, searching, must never stop; the mind must keep flexible in order to lose nothing, to acquire any knowledge that can aid our mission.... Immobility, arrested development bring decadence; a beauty, fully unfolded is ready to perish. So let us not rest on our beautiful past.[59]

Let us accept the invitation to probe the depths of the *Goals and Criteria* that they might be prophetic orientations leading us to hope, a hope that believes in the goodness of each person, a hope that believes in the goodness of humanity, a hope that believes in and trusts the love of the Heart of God.[60]

---

[59] Society of the Sacred Heart General Chapter 2000 Introduction, (Amiens, France, August 2000) p. 14.
[60] Letter to the Society of the Sacred Heart, August 13, 1912, in Margaret Williams, RSCJ, *The Society of the Sacred Heart* (London: Darton, Longman & Todd, 1978) 158.

Foundational Principles

1. In the *Goals and Criteria,* the Society of the Sacred Heart defines the mission of the school as part of the Society's educational mission in the Catholic Church.
2. Each school is accountable to the Society through the Sacred Heart Commission on Goals for adherence to the *Goals and Criteria.*
3. Each school's Board of Trustees and Administration establish and uphold policies that are consistent with the *Goals and Criteria.*
4. The school allocates its resources to support each Goal and its Criteria.
5. The school is in compliance with professional standards as stated by accrediting agencies.

Goal I: Schools of the Sacred Heart commit themselves to educate to a personal and active faith in God.

1. Rooted in the love of Jesus Christ, the school promotes a personal relationship with God and fosters the spiritual lives of its members.
2. The school seeks to form its students in the attitudes of the heart of Jesus expressed in respect, compassion, forgiveness and generosity.
3. The entire school program explores one's relationship to God, to self, to others, and to all creation.
4. Opening themselves to the transforming power of the Spirit of God, members of the school community engage in personal and communal prayer, reflection and action.

5. The entire school program affirms that there is meaning and value in life and fosters a sense of hope in the individual and in the school community.
6. The school fosters inter-religious acceptance and dialogue by educating to an understanding of and deep respect for the religions of the world.
7. The school presents itself to the wider community as a Christ-centered institution and as an expression of the mission of the Society of the Sacred Heart.

Goal II: Schools of the Sacred Heart commit themselves to educate to a deep respect for intellectual values.

1. The school develops and implements a curriculum based on the *Goals and Criteria*, educational research and ongoing evaluation.
2. The school provides a rigorous education that incorporates all forms of critical thinking and inspires a life-long love of learning.
3. The school program develops aesthetic values and the creative use of the imagination.
4. The faculty utilizes a variety of teaching and learning strategies that recognizes the individual needs of the students.
5. The school provides ongoing professional development for faculty and staff.
6. Members of the school community model and teach ethical and respectful use of technology.

Goal III: Schools of the Sacred Heart commit themselves to educate to a social awareness which impels to action.

1. The school educates to a critical consciousness that leads its total community to analyze and reflect on the values of society and to act for justice.
2. The school offers all its members opportunities for direct service and advocacy and instills a life-long commitment to service.
3. The school is linked in a reciprocal manner with ministries among people who are poor, marginalized and suffering from injustice.

4. In our multicultural world, the school prepares and inspires students to be active, informed, and responsible citizens locally, nationally, and globally.
5. The school teaches respect for creation and prepares students to be stewards of the earth's resources.

Goal IV: Schools of the Sacred Heart commit themselves to educate to the building of community as a Christian value.

1. The school implements an ongoing plan for educating both adults and students in the heritage and mission of Sacred Heart education.
2. The school promotes a safe and welcoming environment in which each person is valued, cared for and respected.
3. Adult members of the school model and teach skills needed to build community and practice clear, direct and open communication.
4. The school has programs that teach the principles of nonviolence, conflict resolution and peacemaking.
5. The school makes a deliberate effort to recruit students and employ faculty and staff of diverse races, ethnicities and backgrounds.
6. The financial aid program effectively supports socioeconomic diversity.
7. The school participates actively in the national and international networks of Sacred Heart schools.

Goal V: Schools of the Sacred Heart commit themselves to educate to personal growth in an atmosphere of wise freedom.

1. All members of the school community show respect, acceptance and concern for themselves and for others.
2. School policies and practices promote self-discipline, responsible decision-making, and accountability.
3. Students grow in self-knowledge and develop self-confidence as they learn to deal realistically with their gifts and limitations.

4. School programs provide for recognizing, nurturing and exercising leadership in its many forms.
5. The school provides opportunities for all members of the community to share their knowledge and gifts with others.
6. All members of the school community take personal responsibility for balance in their lives and for their health and well-being.

The appendix of the 2005 edition includes the Preamble of 1975 and the Introduction of 1990.

49657056R00077

Made in the USA
Middletown, DE
20 October 2017